# *Easy Carving Projects for Kids*

## Robin Edward Trudel

## Linden Publishing
## Fresno

Published by Linden Publishing
2006 South Mary
Fresno, California 93721
559-233-6633 / 800-345-4447

To order another copy of this book, please call
1-800-345-4447.

135798642

Editor: Richard Sorsky
Cover design: James Goold
Photography: Robin Edward Trudel
Design and layout: Maura J. Zimmer

ISBN 13: 978-1-933502-30-4

Printed in China on acid-free paper.

Linden Publishing titles may be purchased in quantity at special discounts for educational, business, or promotional use. To inquire about discount pricing, please refer to the contact information above.

Woodworking is inherently dangerous. Your safety is your responsibility.
Neither Linden Publishing nor the author assume
any responsibility for any injuries or accidents.

Library of Congress Cataloging-in-Publication Data

Trudel, Robin Edward, 1966-
    Easy carving projects for kids / by Robin Edward Trudel.
        p. cm.
    ISBN 978-1-933502-30-4 (pbk. : alk. paper)
    1.  Wood-carving--Juvenile literature.  I. Title.
    TT199.7.T793 2010
    736'.4--dc22

                        2009053698

# TABLE OF CONTENTS

Table of Contents

# INTRODUCTION

## A CALL TO ACTION

A quick survey of medical research will reveal concerns with the mental and physical health of our children. Children, as well as adults, suffer from a dearth of physical activity. The modern enemy of children in North America is, simply put, the couch. While I am not suggesting carving as a replacement for riding a bike, anything that inspires mental and physical activity should be encouraged.

If you're a parent, I'm sure you've heard the plaintive paean of "I'm bored." It is far too easy for some children to get locked into the cycle of school, home, homework, electronic entertainment, bed, start again. Television, video games, and such have their places, but they should not be a way of life.

The interested researcher can also find statistics supporting the idea that kids involved in structured activities tend to be more successful in general. I believe that although they may have less opportunity to be bored, the very nature of a highly structured life may inhibit their ability to creatively entertain themselves.

My family was not wealthy, but there was never a shortage of creative materials. I fondly remember an uncle who gave us an enormous roll of butcher paper. There was so much paper we didn't have to worry about it ever running out. The sheer amount of paper inspired creativity. Once my siblings and I made a 6-foot paper airplane, simply because we could. That roll of butcher paper taught me lessons in art, physics, and countless other things.

Introducing a child to creative endeavors can open whole worlds of possibilities. In an effort to shelter our children, we may have inadvertently diminished their desire to "do" in an effort to keep them safe. We must take a deep breath and allow our children to spread their wings a bit.

In my first book, *Carving for Kids*, I described a favorite incident from childhood involving a big cardboard box and some creativity. I was raised in a culture of "make." My parents helped me make my first superhero cape. It long outlasted the thin plastic ones of my classmates. While theirs fell apart in November, mine lasted long enough to be incorporated into play well into the following summer.

I quite clearly remember thinking that if a cape was possible, why not other props? At that time we had a scroll saw and an abundant source of pine boards and plywood. All sorts of wonders came out of these. It is this culture of "make" and "do" that I hope to inspire you to awaken in your children.

Giving children not just the fundamental skills of creation, but the ability to visualize and the confidence to make those visualizations real is intensely empowering.

There should be more to life than an endless cycle of sleep-work-consume-repeat. Each of us is capable of contributing to the body of human knowledge every day. If you intend your children to be productive, you must lead by example.

Much of this book was written on the train between Boston and Lowell while I commuted to and from work. As the other passengers read or dozed, I created. I continued to work my full-time job and assisted my wife raising our children. I maintained my habit of reading two or three fictional works at a time and I perused innumerable nonfiction works. I won a small pile of medals from taekwondo competitions on two continents. I participated in at least three martial arts demonstrations. I earned the Presidential Gold Medal for Fitness. I developed, wrote, and produced a series for our local access cable channel. Our family discovered geocaching and incorporated that into our busy lives. We managed a couple of small vacations. We planned, catered, and participated in the wedding of our eldest daughter and hosted a number of dinner parties. I think we slept at some point, but you'd have to confirm that with my wife.

People ask my wife and me, "How do you do it?" Our answer is simply, "How do you not do it?"

My children see the examples my wife and I provide and the desire to create and be productive has become part of their lives. We are gratified each time we see them working on ongoing projects.

In this book, I propose you use the medium of wood to communicate this lesson. Readily available, recyclable, and renewable, it has protected, warmed, fed, and delighted mankind for millennia.

There is something supremely satisfying about using tools to shape wood, to see something that existed only in your mind begin to take form. Yet, even as you impose your will upon the wood, you will find the wood shaping you as well. It's not hard to see metaphors for our lives in this give-and-take. People who can create feel empowered. People who feel empowered are less likely to be victims and are more likely to take steps to improve their lives and communities.

It is our duty as parents and mentors to share these lessons with the younger members of our community. Be an agent of change. Break the cycle of unimaginative consumerism and be a teacher of "make" and "do."

## You as Mentor

If we accept this duty, we must be prepared to fulfill it. The teacher must be in a patient mental state and not rushed. Take the time to prepare the project in advance; lay out the appropriate tools. Put all unsafe tools out of reach and out of sight, which includes turning power tools off and verifying they are unplugged.

My hope is that this book will serve as a guideline for the creation of projects rather than be an exhaustive step-by-step guide. Certainly, there are plenty of instructions for those that want to reproduce the projects exactly as I've shown here. However, I caution against forcing a child to use a particular design. There are many projects in this book that, as presented, are for older children. These projects could be re-designed for age-appropriate tools for younger children. It is important for the child to grasp the basics, but at least as important is encouraging the child to use those skills to realize their idea.

It is fine to be goal oriented, but as the mentor, keep focused on the real goal, namely the inspiration of the creative act in the child. Leave sufficient time and space so that your work together can be successful. Deadlines and a hurried pace are a recipe for frustration.

Then, of course, there is the apathetic or reluctant child. As an instructor in taekwondo, I've seen some children who are only participating because their parents want them to be there. There is little point in demanding that an unwilling child participate in an activity. These children may not be able to see the benefits of the activity for its own sake and will need incentive to participate.

There are a few other lessons I've learned as a teacher. Be careful to correct and not dwell on criticism. A useful critique with encouragement towards improvement is a good motivator. Lead by example to set the tone. If you're feeling frustrated, chances are so is your student and it might be time to put the project aside. Repetition is a powerful teacher and I encourage you to repeat as many of the projects in this book as often as you like.

## TOOLS OF THE TRADE

As a martial artist, I've managed to rescue hundreds and hundreds of board feet of wood used for breaking during tests and demonstrations. The vast majority of projects in this book have been made from that wood. Check with your local martial arts studios and you might find that they are only too happy to help you rescue the wood from their dumpster.

The projects are broken into three groups, by approximate age.

### GROUP ONE: 4–8

Sanding sticks and stamping tools are well within the dexterity range for these children and with supervision are reasonably safe.

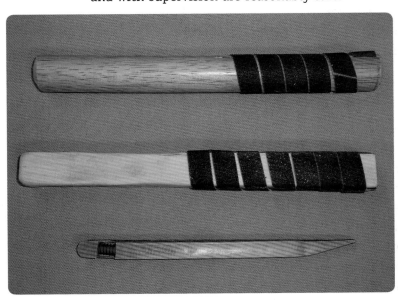

Three sanding sticks are generally sufficient.

A round stick, from a ½ or ¾ inch dowel about 8 inches long.

A square stick, measuring ¾ x ¾ x 8 inches.

A detail stick that may be purchased commercially, or cut from a board.

These sticks can be wrapped in sandpaper, or in the case of the round and square sticks, the top can be sawn and a narrow sanding belt wrapped around the stick.

Stamping tools can be made from various shaped steel nails or can be purchased from carving or leather working suppliers. To make a cross-hatched stamp, clamp a cut steel nail in a vice and cut the lines across the head with a hacksaw or use a diamond blade in a rotary tool.

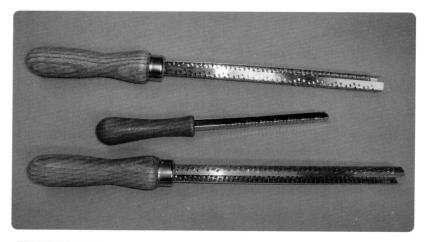

### GROUP TWO: 9–12

I have been a big fan of Microplane tools since I did some testing of their first products back in the 1990s. Although similar results can be obtained with rasps, the Microplane products do not clog as much and are less likely to frustrate young carvers. I suggest a round, a square, and a flat Microplane. Some of the projects for this age group require a knife and/ or a v-tool. Please do consider carefully if the carver has enough dexterity and strength to use these tools before attempting these projects.

### GROUP THREE: 13 AND UP

These carvers need supervision, but they have the dexterity to use knives and gouges. It is an old wives' tale that a dull knife is safer. A dull knife requires more strength, which increases the danger that the tool will slip and injure the carver. Anyone using a sharp tool should be wearing a carving glove on the free hand and should take the utmost caution to be sure that body parts are not in the way of a tool that might slip.

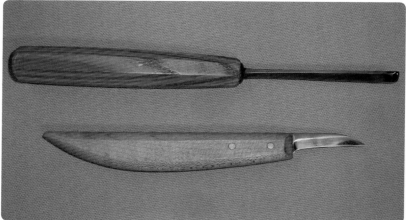

Basic knife cuts:

Most knife carving consists of three basic knife cuts. These three techniques are sufficient to create the most complex of knife carvings.

The stop cut is made by pushing the knife blade directly into the wood. This cut creates a "stop" for one of the next two cuts.

The paring cut is similar to what you would do if you were peeling a vegetable with a paring knife. The knife is held in the curl of the four fingers. The blade faces towards the carver. The thumb is braced against the carving, away from the path of the knife. As the fingers curl inward, the knife is pressed into the wood removing a chip of varying thickness.

The levering cut is the opposite of the paring cut. The blade faces away from the carver. As it is placed on the wood, the thumb of the hand not holding the knife pushes on the back of the blade.

In many of the projects in this book, basic chip carving techniques and terms are used, so they are introduced here.

The three cut removes a triangular section of wood. Two stop cuts are made into the wood forming two sides of a triangle. The third cut is a paring or levering cut depending on the room available and the grain direction. It starts from one side of the open side of the triangle and is carved across so that the knife blade carves up to one of the two stop cuts. If done correctly, a single chip will pop free. This technique is not just limited to chip carving, but can be found in many of the projects.

The six cut removes what looks like an inverted pyramid from the wood. Three stop cuts are made, each starting with the knife tip at the center. The cuts extend into the corners of the pyramid. The second three cuts are either levering or paring cuts as space and grain allows. These three cuts are like the final cut of the three cut and they each remove a chip.

## A Few Last Notes

For the sake of clarity, at times some of the hand positions that are shown are not particularly safe. Do take caution in the placement of the carver's hands to prevent injury.

Have a first aid kit handy. As careful as you would like to be, an accident is possible. Generally, antiseptic spray, Band-Aids and an antibiotic ointment will take care of most little nicks. Dr. Augustus Luparelli, a former co-worker and an accomplished woodworker, recommends keeping a baby diaper in the first aid kit of a workshop. In case of a more serious injury, the diaper can be taped around the injured area and will stay in place while the person is transported for medical attention.

The best place to teach children may not be in your workshop. The temptation to push buttons, flick switches, and change settings on power tools can be overwhelming. If your workshop is the only choice, unplug all the power tools and throw drop cloths over unneeded tools.

I have found it helpful, especially when working on projects with multiple parts, to use a cardboard soda box to keep everything together from session to session. It's also handy for placing parts while you are preparing them for the carver.

Rubberized shelf lining is excellent to protect work surfaces and prevent sliding. You will see it is featured in many of the photos but it does not replace proper clamping for safety. It is certainly not suitable to hold work in place for use with power tools. Do consider the needs of the project. Proper clamping frees up your hands and allows more control over the tools and reduces the potential for injury.

As I mentioned in *Carving for Kids*, three of my four children are challenged, to various degrees. This has not prevented any of them from woodcarving and in some cases having photos of their work published in the *New England Wood Carver's Newsletter*. Two of my children have taught woodcarving to younger carvers and they all look forward to introducing it to my grandson Tai. Simply put, age or developmental differences should not be a barrier to introducing children to wood sculpture.

You are the best judge of your carver's capabilities. My categorizations of the projects are based on my personal experience with children's interest and abilities at certain ages. Nearly every one of these projects can be made more accessible by modifying the projects to suit the skills of the carver. The general rule is the less developed the carver's motor skills, the more prep work must be completed to make the project possible and safe for them.

*Robin Edward Trudel*
*November 2009*

# SECTION ONE: KITCHEN AND PARTY

*Everybody loves a party. The preparations can be as exciting as the event itself. The theme of this group of projects is wooden items for cooking and dining, also known as woodenware. Woodenware has an ancient and honored history in North America. Wood was plentiful and most households had the basic tools required for producing much of what they needed. If properly maintained, woodenware can be a versatile and elegant addition to any event and woodenware used for serving deserves special attention.*

*However, wood must be treated differently than ceramic or metal kitchenware. As wood changes shape with humidity, it needs to be protected. Although there are commercial finishes designed for food surfaces, I recommend mineral oil or 100% pure beeswax. Both are safe for ingestion, but both need to be re-applied when the wood becomes dry.*

*I've a fondness for cooking for friends. On many evenings we've collected smiling faces and warm hearts around a table full of dishes inspired by countries from around the world. A deadline, like a party, can also make the production of carved items even more exciting.*

# WOODEN DRINK COASTERS

## Ages 4 to 8

My lovely bride Joyce loves decorative coasters. We have quite a few sets, but the wooden ones seem to outlast the others, either due to their lack of fragility or their natural beauty.

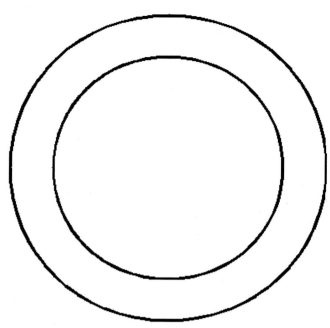

**Project Pattern**

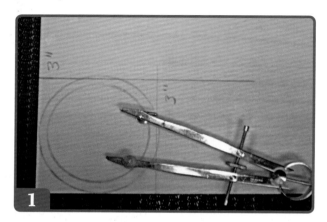

**Lay out the design using a compass.** Set the points 1½-inches apart to draw a 3-inch circle. This will be the line to cut. Reduce the points to 1¼-inches and use the same center to draw a concentric circle.

**Cut the circle using a band, scroll, or other fine-bladed saw.** Use a toothed stamp with a circular outline.

**Since this is the first project, it's recommended to have the carver test his or her technique on scrap wood.** Turn and move the stamp with each strike so the pattern is not regular.

**4**

**After sufficient practice, help the carver to place the stamp just inside the compass line, then strike the stamp.** After completing a circle inside the scribed pencil line, erase the line so that it is not visible in the final carving.

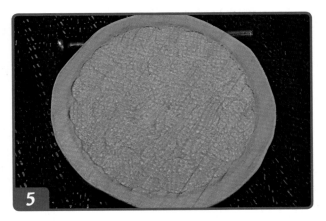

**5**

After erasing the line, stamp the center so that the entire interior circle is stamped down.

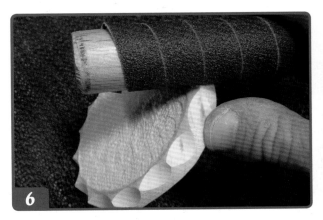

**6**

**Show the carver how to create a scalloped edge using the round sanding stick.** Keep it at a 45-degree angle and remove the wood to a depth of about ¼ inch.

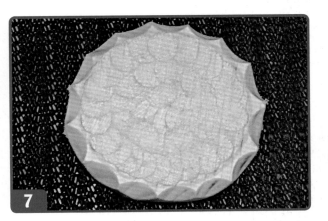

**7**

Consistent depth and angle will yield a pleasant-looking result.

The coaster can be finished in a number of ways. A thin coat of mineral oil will make the coasters safe for the dishwasher. Let the wood dry thoroughly on an absorbent surface, like a paper plate or towel. Do not use newspaper as the print will transfer. If a pad is required for the bottom, self-adhesive cork or felt may be added, but then the coasters will need to be hand washed. An enthusiastic carver should be able to make a set of six over several short sessions.

# NAPKIN RINGS

## *Ages 4 to 8*

Generally I don't use cloth napkins when we're entertaining, but when we do, it signals the commemoration of a special event. Napkin rings inscribed with the purpose for a commemorative dinner can make a nice memento of the evening.

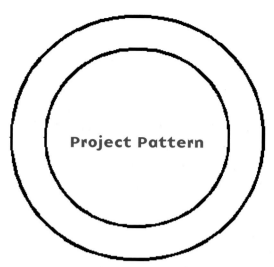

**Project Pattern**

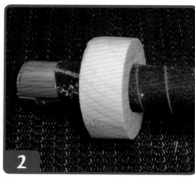

**1**

**The pattern for the napkin ring is laid out much the same as the coaster.** Select a clear piece of ¾-inch white pine. Set the points of the compass 1 inch apart to scribe a 2-inch circle. Using the same center, reduce the arms to ½-inch apart to mark the hollow center.

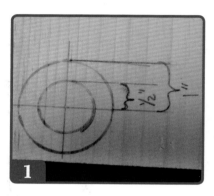

**2**

**Drill or scroll saw out the center and then cut the outside of the napkin ring.** Sand the outside of the napkin ring and let the carver start the project by using the round sanding stick to smooth the inside. It is important that the inside be smooth so the napkins do not snag.

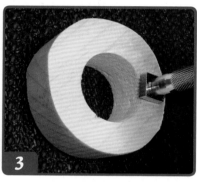

**3**

**Using a toothed stamp, stamp both sides of the napkin ring.**

**4**

**Alternately, direct the carver to create a pattern using the stamp by leaving some areas unstamped.**

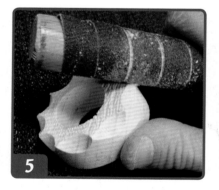

**5**

**As before with the coaster, show the carver how to create a scalloped edge.** Use the round sanding stick at a 45-degree angle and remove the wood to a depth of about ¼ inch. Be sure to create the scalloped edge on both sides of the napkin ring.

**6**

**Finish with a light coat of polyurethane spray.** If oil is used on the rings it may stain the napkins.

# TRIVETS

## Ages 4 to 8

Trivets seem to have fallen out of fashion these days, but for informal dining it's easier to bring pots right to the table than to dirty serving bowls. In these cases, a decorative trivet hanging in a convenient place can be pressed into service.

Transfer the outline of the cutting board onto a straight-grained piece of pine ¾ inch thick and at least 6 x 8 inches in size.

**Project Pattern**

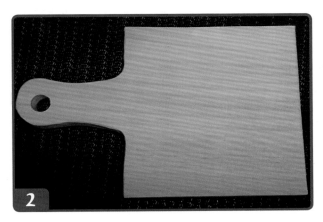

**Cut the outline using a scroll or band saw.** Set the points of the compass 2 inches apart and scribe a 4-inch circle in the center of the board.

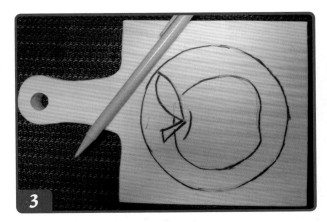

**Transfer the design into the center of the circle.** This design will use the square toothed stamp, a smooth stamp, and a round toothed stamp.

Have the carver start with the round punch and outline the inside of the circle, remembering to rotate the stamp to create an even pattern.

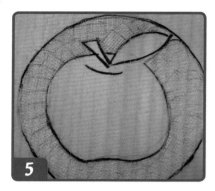
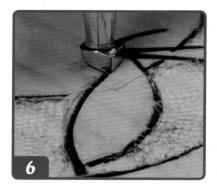
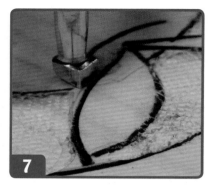

**5**
**Switch to the square punch to outline the apple, the stem and the leaf.** The smooth stamp will be used to separate the details of the stem, leaf and apple.

**6**
**Set the smooth stamp against the edge of the leaf and stamp the apple lower.**

**7**
**Continue along the leaf until it is raised above the apple.** Also, perform the same work on the side of the stem to raise it above the apple. The work between the leaf and the stem will be tricky for all but the most patient.

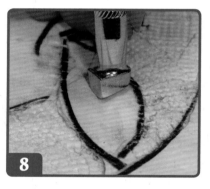
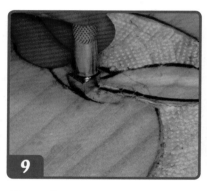
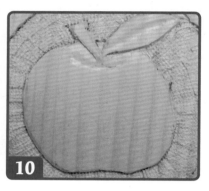

**8**
**Use the smooth stamp to create a shadow along the leaf center.**

**9**
**Above the curve representing the indentation where the stem is attached, create a shadow by stamping.**

**10**
**With the stamping complete, erase as much of the pencil lines as possible.**

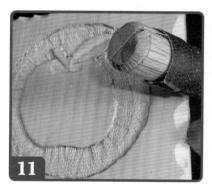
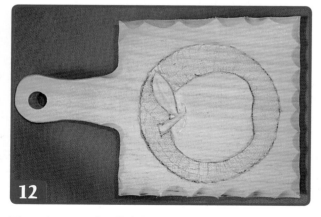

**11**
**Using the round sanding stick, create a scalloped edge around the trivet.** Holding the sanding stick at about a 45-degree angle, remove wood to about a ¼ inch depth.

**12**
**The trivet can be finished with a light coat of mineral oil.** When the trivet is washed, the oil may need to be refreshed from time to time.

# BREAD BOARD

## Ages 9 to 12

As often as we entertain, we are invited to dinner events at friends' houses. At some of these events the hosts insist that there is nothing for us to bring. Instead of going empty handed, one of these bread boards with a nice loaf of bread or wedge of cheese is a nice thank you for the invitation.

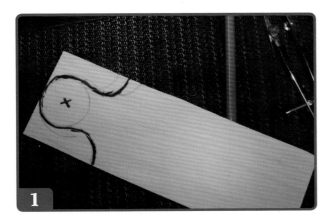

**Select a clear piece of 4 x 8 x ¼ inch white pine.** Set the points of the compass 1 inch apart and draw a 2-inch circle near the end of the board. Place an X at the center. Measure 6 inches from the other end and make a light mark. Mark a reverse curve from this mark up to the circle. This will define the shape of the handle.

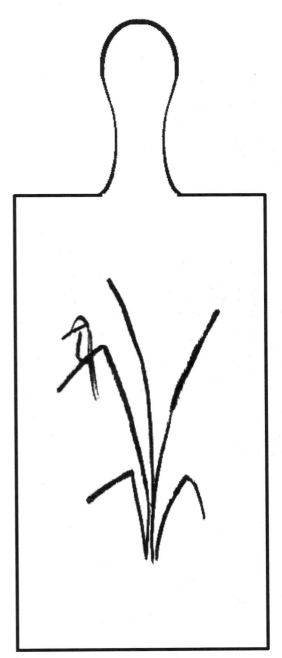

Project Pattern

**Saw out the handle of the cutting board and drill a hanging hole where the X was marked earlier.** Sand all surfaces smooth.

**3**

**Layout the design or transfer the pattern onto the wood.** Alternatively, photocopy the pattern and use temporary spray adhesive to affix it to the board.

The entire project consists of repeating the same two cuts. The results of using a knife are preferred, but if the cuts are too inconsistent, the design can be executed using a v-tool. If the carver is not ready to use sharp tools, the pattern may be stamped in using a flat screwdriver and a mallet.

If the carver wishes to practice the cuts first, draw a curved line similar to the design on a piece of scrap pine and let them try the two cuts described below. At a 30-degree angle to the wood, insert about a $\frac{1}{32}$ of an inch into the wood and maintaining the angle, create a single curved cut.

*Section One: Kitchen and Party*

**4**

**5**

**Turn the board around and make a second cut angled into the first.** If performed correctly, a single long chip will be freed as the cut is completed.

**With one of the lines of the designs completed, direct the carver to carefully work over the entire design.** Be aware that some of the curves on the bird are very tight and must be done carefully.

**6**

When the scene is complete, coat the board lightly with mineral oil and let it dry on an absorbent surface, like paper towels or paper plates.

# DECORATIVE SERVING PLATTER

## Ages 9 to 12

This platter features a quote from the poet Omar Khayyam. The design was inspired by a reconciliatory gift I was asked to create by one-half of a couple with whom I am acquainted. They had had a falling out due to a third party and this person wanted to remind their beloved how important they were to them.

**Project Pattern**

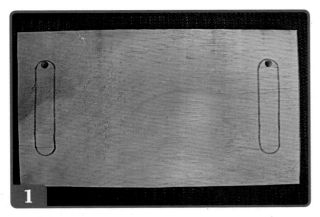

**Select a piece of white pine 24 x 12 x ¾ inches.** Transfer the pattern for the handles and drill pilot holes for the scroll saw blade.

Scroll saw out the handle holes. The smoother the board, the crisper the letters will look. Sand with progressively finer paper until all surfaces are smooth. Sand the sharp edges of the board as well. Using a sanding stick, or rolled-up sandpaper, sand the inside of the handles. When all the surfaces feel smooth, wipe the board off with a slightly damp cloth, let dry and then sand one more time with the finest sandpaper.

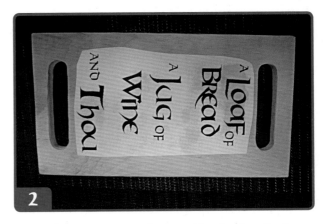

Use a spray adhesive to attach a copy of the pattern to the platter or use some other method to transfer the pattern.

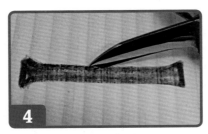

**Select a piece of 3 x 6 x ¾ inch wood to practice these sample letters.** Sketch the letters onto the wood.

**Carve the capital "I" or lower-case "l" by making a long, angled cut,** working from the top of the letter to the bottom.

**5**

**Make a stop cut across the bottom of the letter.** Make another stop cut across the top of the letter.

**6**

**Make another long cut from the bottom to the top and a single chip should be freed.**

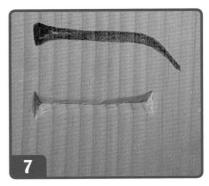

**7**

When complete the letter should resemble the photo.

**8**

**The "J" is carved in a similar fashion to the "I".** Working from the top, make a long cut down to the tip of the "J".

**9**

**Turn the board around and carve from the bottom to the top of the "J" on the other side.** Add a stop cut across the top of the "J" to free the last of the wood.

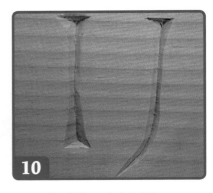

**10**

Here the "I" and the "J" are complete.

**11**

**To carve the "E", start with the middle part of the "E" and make an angled cut from the tip back to the curved part of the letter.**

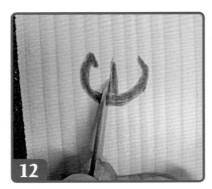

**12**

Switch sides and make a second cut opposite the first.

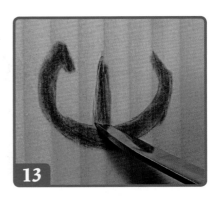

**13**

Make a stop cut to free the chip.

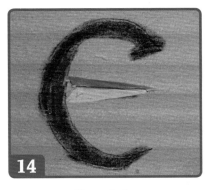

**14**

The center line of the "E" complete.

**15**

Starting from the point at the bottom of the "E" make a cut all the way around the outside of the "E."

**16**

**Start from the bottom point of the "E" and carve a line around the outside to the top.** As with the other letters, make a stop cut to free the last chip.

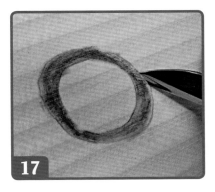

**17**

**To start the "O", cut in the outside of the letter first,** then the inside, similar to the letter "C."

**18**

Here, the practice letters are complete.

**19**

**If the letter crosses the grain, sometimes a center cut creates a better result.** Make a stop cut the length of the letter. Create a stop cut across the top of the letter. Make another stop cut across the bottom.

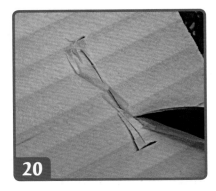

**20**

Now make the angled cuts on both sides of the letter.

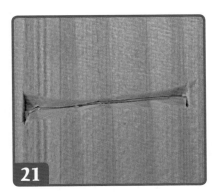

**21**

The letter completed.

**22**

**The practice letters are complete.** Now begin work upon the platter. Start on the right leg of the "A" and make an angled cut on the outside from top to bottom.

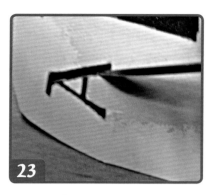

**23**

Reverse the angle and make a matching angled cut from top to bottom on the inside of the right leg. A single chip should pop free.

**24**

Make a short angled cut at the top of the serif on the top of the "A." Reversing the angle, make an angled cut at the bottom of the serif to pop free another chip.

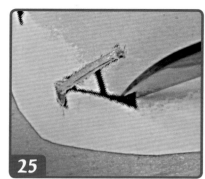

**25**

Start at the top of the inside of the thinner left leg of the "A" with an angled cut, turning outward to the serif at the inside of the leg.

**26**

Make another cut on the outside of the left leg down to the bottom of the letter. A stop cut across the bottom should free the chip.

**27**

Make another cut across the bottom of the bar at the center of the letter.

**28**

The chip should come free with this second cut at the reverse angle, as wood carved away for the legs of the "A" serve as stop cuts.

The first letter is completed.

**29**

Begin the "L" with an angled cut at the bottom of the letter starting at the point.

**30**

Reverse the blade and make a cut from the other side.

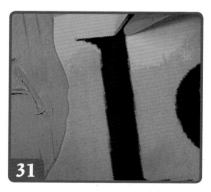

**31**

Make a stop cut from the point of the serif to the front of the letter.

**32**

Starting at the outside of the vertical part of the "L" from the bottom, make an angled cut up toward the top of the letter.

**33**

Again, reverse the angle of the blade and carve from bottom to top.

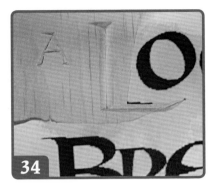

**34**

Now two letters are complete.

**35**

Begin the "O" with an angled cut halfway around the outside, as on our sample piece. In this font, the "O" becomes narrow so the best results will be obtained by carving two crescents.

**36**

Reverse the angle of the blade and carve the inside of the "O."

**37**

With one crescent complete, begin the other.

**38**

The second cut on that side of the letter should pop out another chip and finish the letter.

**39**

Three letters complete. Start the "A" with a stop cut at the bottom of the vertical part of the letter.

**40**

Then make a stop cut across the top.

**41**

Make an angled cut along the length on the inside and outside of this vertical part, as before.

**42**

Similar to the "O," make the angled cut on the inside of the letter. Then reverse the angle to cut the outside of the letter.

**43**

Four letters complete.

**44**

Begin the "F" with an angled cut across the top of the letter. Stop cut the end of the upper part of the "F."

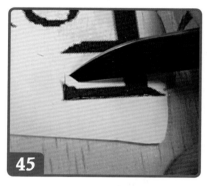

**45**

Starting from the end of the last stop cut, make an angled cut to the vertical part of the letter.

**46**

When the third cut is complete, the top of the letter should resemble the photo. Starting from the bottom of the serif, on the outside of the letter make an angled cut up to the top serif.

Then make the complimentary cut on the other side, working from top to bottom.

**47**

Here, two parts of the "F" are complete.

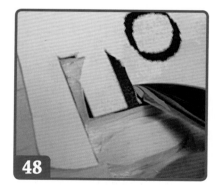

**48**

Start the last part of the "F" by carving from the tip of the lower bar of the letter and carve to the vertical part.

**49**

Make one final cut from the body of the letter, to the tip to release the wood chip.

**50**

Here, five letters are complete.

**51**

This letter is carved the same as the earlier "O," but keep in mind it is smaller.

**52**

Another "F," this time start with the vertical portion. Be sure to carve both sides to release the chip.

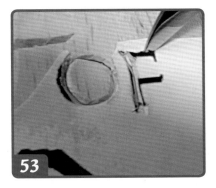

**53**

For the upper line of the "F," make an angled cut across the top.

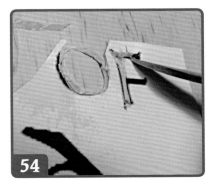

**54**

Make an angled cut across the bottom.

**55**

Third, make the stop cut at the end which will release the chip. Repeat the process with the lower line of the "F."

**56**

The first line completed. Using the techniques from the practice piece and the first line, proceed with each letter.

**57**

In the fourth line, two three-cut chips were removed to provide a dot for the letter "I."

*(right)* **The completed project.** A couple of coats of matte or satin polyurethane will seal the board nicely, but if the back is to be used for cutting, or warm dishes are likely to be placed on it, a food-safe, oil-based finish is recommended.

**58**

## SALAD HANDS

### Ages 9 to 12

Salad spoons are frequently pressed into service at parties to be used as spare serving spoons. These salad hands have one purpose by design and thereby they are more likely to be available. Certainly any highly figured wood would enhance this project. Olive wood is particularly effective, but it is only recommended for the most persistent carvers, as its density makes for difficult work.

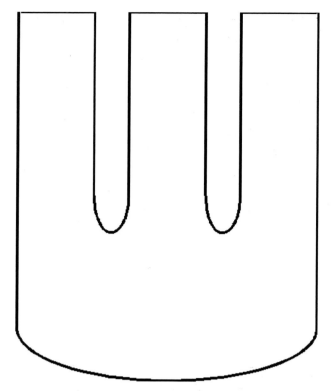

**Project Pattern**

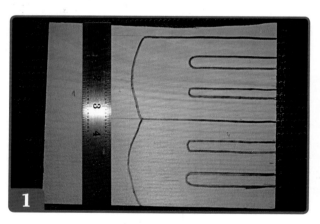

**1**

**Select a piece of wood at least 6 x 6 x ¾ inches.** The wood should be clear and free of knots with straight grain. Transfer the design onto the wood, orienting the fingers of the salad hands parallel with the grain.

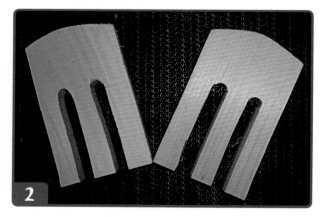

**2**

**Take the piece to the band, scroll, or coping saw and cut out the blanks.**

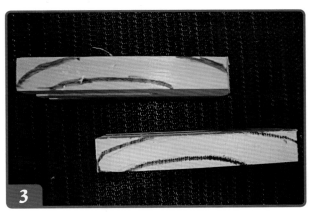

Transfer the side view onto the sides of the salad hands.

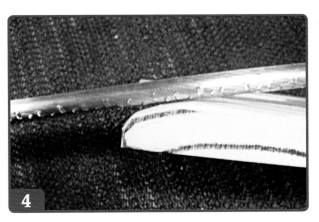

**Using the flat Microplane, relieve the fronts of the fingers with long even strokes.** Be sure that the wood is removed evenly across all the fingers. Smoother cuts with the rasp will minimize the amount of sanding required later. Remove the wood from the back of the salad hand using the same tool. Be sure to perform the tasks on both hands.

Use the same tool to make the underside of the hand concave.

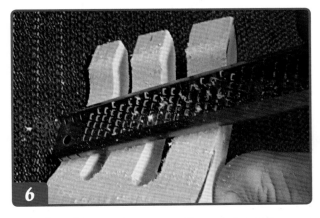

**As before, be sure to remove the wood evenly.** Remove wood from the underside of the other hand as well. Now use the round Microplane to relieve all the outside edges of the hands. Round the sharp corners at the back of both hands. Relieve the corners of the fingers.

Surface the hands entirely, including between the fingers. All surfaces should be rounded, leaving no trace of squareness or saw marks. Sand both hands to a glassy finish, using fine sandpaper.

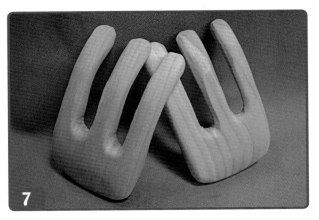

With regular oiling, these salad hands should last a lifetime.

# PLACE CARD HOLDER

## Ages 13 and up

In my family during the holidays there was never assigned seating, so place card holders wouldn't have been useful. However, with the variety of dishes that were served, a holder for a card describing the dishes would have been welcome. This holder is in the shape of a pineapple that in Western culture is a symbol of hospitality.

**Project Pattern**

**1**

**Select a piece of clear, straight-grained white pine that measures at least 4 x 6 inches.** Transfer the pattern to the wood.

**2**

**Before cutting out the profile, cut a saw kerf into the top of the pineapple.** This slot will hold the card. Cut out the profile using a band, scroll, or coping saw.

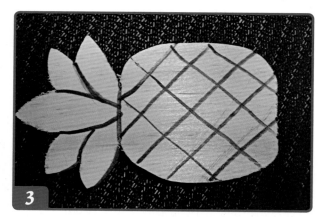

**3**

Draw in the details from the pattern, including the leaves and the crosshatched lines on both sides of the pineapple.

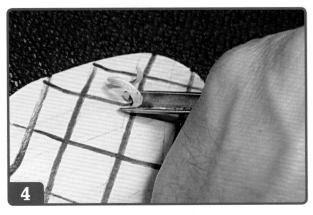

Start with a ⅜-inch v-tool and carve in the cross-hatched lines on the pineapple.

Carve in the lines for the leaves.

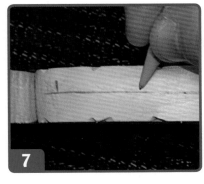

**Any of these v-tool cuts can be done with a knife alone.** Make a cut at about a 30-degree angle in one direction. Turn the carving around, cut the line from the opposite side and a single long chip will be released. Be sure to carve all the lines on both sides of the pineapple.

**Draw a centerline around the blank.** This line represents the highest point that will remain when the edges are relieved. Carve about a 45-degree bevel around the outside of the blank.

**As the crosshatched lines are carved off, be sure to draw them back in.**

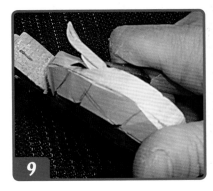

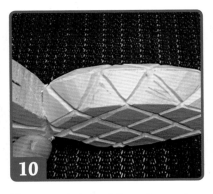

**Relieve the edges all around the fruit, leaving the earlier penciled line as the highest point.** When the lines are re-drawn, be careful to plan them out so they meet their counterparts from the other side. Re-carve the cross-hatched marks when the shaping of the fruit is completed.

**The crosshatched lines here are carved and meet reasonably well with the other side.**

**Using the knife, set the cross-hatched lines in deeper.** First make a stop cut at about a 45-degree angle. Follow the stop cut up with another one on the other side of the line.

**12**

This deepening and widening of the crosshatched lines will result in raised diamond shaped bumps, resembling the skin of a pineapple.

**13**

Draw in the center spines on each of the leaves on both sides of the pineapple. Like the sides of the fruit, these lines serve as reference for the highest point.

**14**

Pare down the sides of each of the leaves. Leave the spine high. Carve from the line at the spine to the centerline drawn earlier around the whole pineapple.

**15**

Here, one side of the pineapple is completed.

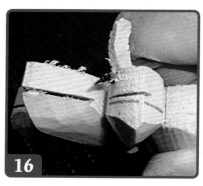

**16**

Begin the work on the other side, again leaving the centerline as the highest point on the side of the leaves. Slow and careful work around the saw kerf will prevent chipping.

**17**

After the carving was complete, the bottom of the pineapple was sanded flat so it would stand correctly. The final carving was painted with thinned acrylics and was given a light coat of polyurethane.

# WINE GLASS HOLDERS

## Ages 13 and up

A simple but amusing problem. You're at a wine tasting or other party where wine is served. You're offered a glass of wine. Then you're offered a tasty treat on a plate. Now you're stuck. You can either go hunting for a convenient end table, or pull one of these wine glass holders out of your pocket.

This wine glass holder design was inspired by a photo I saw of an acquaintance at a wine tasting in France, but since we're carvers here, embellishment is a must.

**Project Pattern**

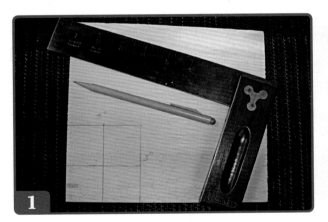

**1** Find a piece of white pine or basswood with a clear, straight-grained area measuring at least **3 x 3 inches.** Lay out a square 3 x 3 inches. Divide this square into 4 equal squares.

**2** Cut out the square using a band or scroll saw. Drill a ½-inch hole at the center point. Sand the entire piece.

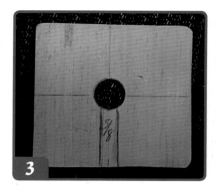

**3**

Working with the grain, measure an area ³/₈-inch wide centered on one of the lines left over from measuring the center of the square.

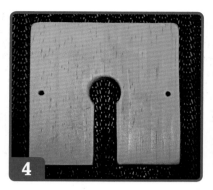

**4**

**Cut along these lines preparing a keyhole-like slot.** One-quarter inch from the edges on the centerline that is perpendicular to the slot, drill ⅛-inch holes.

**5**

**Take one of the wineglasses you intend to use and check the keyhole slot for a fit.** It may need adjusting, involving widening of the hole or slot to accommodate the stem. When it fits, give it a final sanding. Use a plastic eraser to clean any remaining abrasive material.

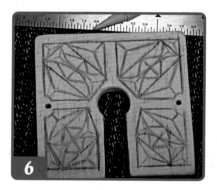

**6**

Transfer the pattern to the piece.

**7**

**This design is repeated in the four corners.** To carve it, the student will be repeating the six-cut chip. Start at one of the corners and make the stop cuts.

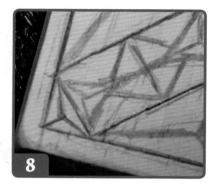

**8**

**The three stop cuts are completed.** Be sure to maintain a consistent depth. Carefully lever out the three chips, again maintaining a consistent depth.

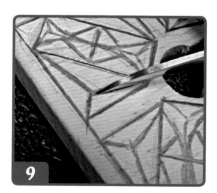

**9**

**Move on to another laid-out six-cut.** This one is larger and will be deeper; however, the stop cuts and angled cuts need to be consistent.

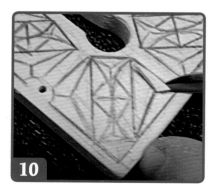

**10**

**The stop cuts completed.** The knife tip is inserted at the same angle as the stop cut that completes the chip. Carve up to it and a single chip will be freed.

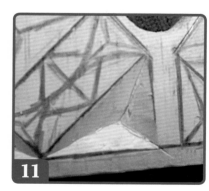

**11**

**Repeating the process two more times completes another six-cut.**

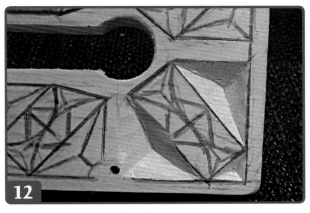

**12**

**Move to the opposite end of that corner and remove the other large six-cuts.** These two six-cuts have slightly curved sides. Carve the chips for the first arc.

**13**

**Once the second arc is finished, this corner of the piece is completed.**

**14**

**Some may find it easier to perform all the stop cuts at once.** Remove all the chips without changing hand positions. The process is left to the carver, but consistency in the depth of the cuts is important.

**15**

**Finish the fourth quadrant to complete the piece.** Use a plastic eraser to remove any extra pencil lines.

The carving should be finished with several coats of matte or flat polyurethane to prevent wine stains. After the finish is dry, thread nylon cord through the two holes long enough so that the wood and the glass it contains rests comfortably in the center of one's chest.

# Section Two: Camping/Picnic

*Weather permitting, a picnic is an inexpensive and easy way to get the family out of the house and away from the television. Fortunately, in most of North America, wooded areas are just a short drive or bus ride away.*

*Geocaching is a treasure-hunting game that relies on information from an Internet site and Global Positioning Satellites. One of the most popular sites is geocaching.com, where players register to get clues. Volunteers who are geocachers themselves hide weatherproof containers containing a log and some trinkets on public property and record the GPS coordinates. They then fill out a form on geocaching.com to publish the availability of the geocache.*

*Geocachers download the information from geocaching.com, program it into their portable GPS unit and go treasure hunting.*

*I originally investigated this as a reward activity for my son and was amazed to find hundreds of geocaches within a short drive of our home on Windy Hill. There have been many wondrous hours spent finding and exploring nearly forgotten pieces of town, state, and federal properties. We've followed clues to long-abandoned fire towers, farms, ski hills, and all manner of wilderness.*

*When we find a geocache, we sign the log, take one of the trinkets, leave a trinket and re-hide the cache. Small carvings make excellent geocache trade items.*

*Motivated by the lure of treasure, our family has discovered dozens and dozens of town and state properties hidden just a few miles from where I've lived my whole life.*

Most of the projects in this chapter can be created using found wood. These projects can serve as useful items as well as wonderful mementos of a family afternoon.

Just as fortunate is that these wooded areas are full of windblown, downed branches and limbs that can serve as raw material for many simple projects. A coworker of mine related to me a story of a picnic that he and his family enjoyed in his youth. As I recall, his father had forgotten the silverware and utensils and they thought the day was lost. His father, not to be defeated by such a setback, got his children to round up some branches and they set about making what they needed.

Found wood can be of very "hit or miss" quality. Driftwood often has sand particles embedded in it and needs careful cleaning and brushing or it will dull carving tools quickly. Look for dry branches. When the branch is struck against a hard surface, a solid sounding clunk should be heard. If it's a dull thud, the wood may have begun to rot and may not be suitable.

Inspect the wood for insects and discard it if borers are found. I once found a very interesting branch with a hole in it and brought it home only to discover to my horror that there were borers in it. I only discovered this when I went to my work area and heard their progeny chomping through my wood.

Lastly, please do not take branches off live trees for carving. First, the branches will be wet and not suitable for carving. Second and more importantly, we are the stewards of our wild places and if we want to preserve them for our young carvers, setting an example by respecting the live trees is a good way to do it.

# CHOPSTICKS AND CHOPSTICK REST

## Ages 4 to 8

As you can imagine, perhaps the easiest utensils to fashion are chopsticks. A suitable branch to use for raw material would be about 1 to 2 inches around and have a good 10 inches of straight wood uninterrupted by knots or flaws. Wood species doesn't matter terribly, but like with all found wood, be careful. Noxious weeds and poisonous plants can sometimes develop quite large limbs. Poison ivy chopsticks would not do much for a picnic.

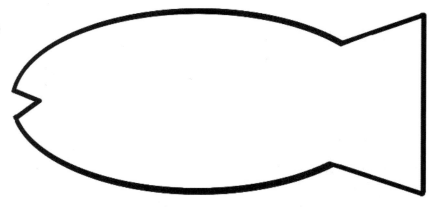

**Project Pattern**

**Select a branch about 1 inch thick that has at least 10 inches of sound, clear wood.** Cut that 10-inch length. Use a hatchet or pocketknife blade to split the branch in half lengthwise. Split one of the two halves lengthwise, making two quarters. Split one of the quarters lengthwise making two more pieces. Discard the piece with more bark. Split the selected piece one more time. If the grain is straight, it should split evenly.

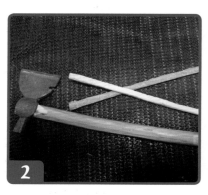

Once the sticks are split, turn them over to the carver to sand smooth while you prepare the chopstick rest.

The chopsticks may be sanded round or left square as long as the finished surface is smooth.

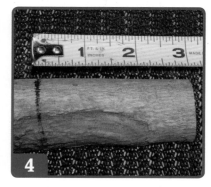

Select another branch about 1-inch thick that has at least 3 inches of sound, clear wood.

**5**

Use a hatchet or pocketknife blade to split the branch in half lengthwise. Set aside one of the pieces to make a second chopstick rest, if desired.

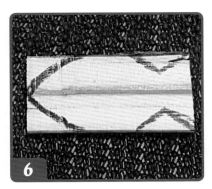

**6**

Transfer the pattern onto the flat side of the chosen half of the branch. Instruct the carver to use the square sanding stick to remove the wood from the area where the body of the fish meets the tail.

**7**

Once one side of the fish is sanded thoroughly, the carver should do the same to the other. With the tail shaped, the carver should sand the sides of the head so that they taper towards the mouth.

**8**

When the outline has been sanded into shape, the carver should sand beneath the head and tail to create a convex curve that is slightly flattened where it rests on the table.

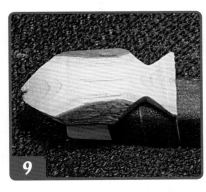

**9**

Here the shaping of the bottom is complete.

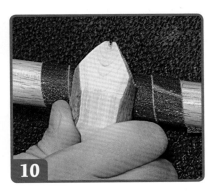

**10**

To match the convex bottom, use the round sanding stick to sand a concave curve across the top of the fish.

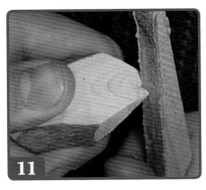

**11**

With the corner of the detail sanding stick, make a few quick strokes at the point of the head to form a mouth.

**12**

The entire fish should be sanded smooth.

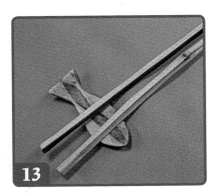

**13**

A few drops of mineral oil are enough to finish both items. The oil should be reapplied as necessary.

# DECORATED WALKING STICK

## Ages 4 to 8

Walk with a child for 10 minutes and they will find a stick to carry. Sometimes these wind-fallen branches become treasured mementos of childhood. Somewhere among my 'stuff' I have several walking sticks from various youthful excursions. If your carver wants to decorate their stick, the first decision is bark on, or bark off. Depending on the branch, the bark might stay on. If you strip off the bark, try not to damage the dark, thin layer between the bark and the growth rings. When the carver uses a sanding stick or rasp, it will take minimal effort to abrade away this material and the stark contrast produced can be incorporated into the design.

**Help the carver find a walking stick about elbow height and approximately 1 inch in diameter.**
There should be at least 6 inches of clear wood toward the end of the stick so that the carver can add some creativity to the stick.

**Ask the carver what they would like to put on the stick.** In this case, my son asked for his name, but other information like date, location, or any other text could be added.

**Project Pattern**

**3**

Show the carver how to use the side of the detail sanding stick to sand through the bark and into the wood to create the vertical lines of the letters or numbers. For angles and horizontal lines, the tip of the detail sanding stick works well.

**4**

Here the first letter is completed. With younger children, remember to stick with block letters drawn as simply as possible.

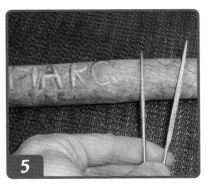

**5**

The next design idea could be accomplished using the detail stick, but if the child has the motor skills to use needle files, much finer details can be created. Use a triangle needle file, or the side of the detail stick, to carve a line around the stick. About a finger-width farther down, carve in a parallel line around the stick.

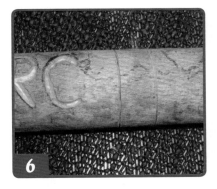

**6**

Here the parallel lines are complete.

**7**

To make a zigzag pattern between the lines, angle the tool at about 45 degrees across the lines and carve a new line.

**8**

Reverse the tool's angle and add another line, continuing around the stick. Plan the last lines carefully so they match up reasonably well. Endless ornamentation can be added to the stick using those simple techniques. Using the round sanding stick, carve a handgrip.

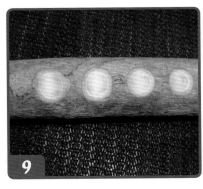

**9**

The four carved spots should closely correspond to the child's hand size.

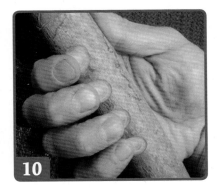

**10**

Here the handgrip is complete. Encourage the child to fill every inch of the stick with their designs.

# A SIMPLE PUZZLE

## Ages 4 to 8

We all remember how interminable family car rides can seem to a young child. While this project would be difficult to do with limited tools on a picnic, it's a great way to occupy a child while they are waiting to leave and a nice little game for them in the car or at the picnic itself.

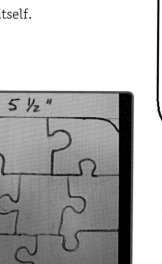

**Project Pattern**

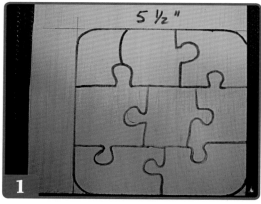

**Start with a piece of straight grained wood like eastern white pine.** Be sure the piece selected is at least 5½ by 5½ inches or has a clean area of that size. Transfer a puzzle design of your own making, such as the above, onto the wood.

**Cut the outline of the puzzle and sand the edges and the side that does not display the puzzle pattern.** On this blank side, transfer the brontosaur pattern.

**Start with the smooth angled stamp.** If this tool is not available, a cut-steel nail head can be ground at an angle and polished to perform the same task.

**Have the carver place the stamp against the edge of the design and stamp around the outside of the brontosaur.** This will create the effect of raising the brontosaur.

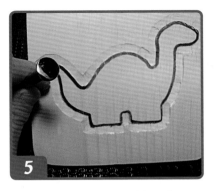

**5**

When the entire outside of the brontosaur is stamped, select a round polished stamp or a large nail head polished for the same purpose.

*(right)* **Assist the carver in stamping down the edge of the stamping that was just done.** This is to soften the outline around the brontosaur.

With the background lowered, select a toothed stamp to texture the brontosaur. The stamped marks will emulate the scaly skin. Remind the carver to turn the tool frequently and use even strokes with the mallet to create the right effect.

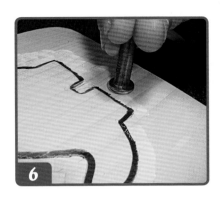

**6**

**7**

When the stamping is complete, the brontosaur should resemble the photo above. Use a flathead screwdriver to set in the mouth. If the strike is too hard, the wood will crumble and the stamp will not leave a clean line.

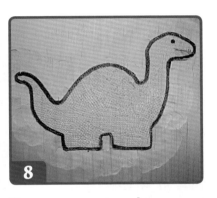

**8**

Use a permanent marker or paint to give the brontosaur an eye.

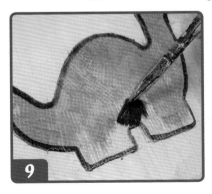

**9**

I used non-toxic watercolors to paint the brontosaur, but if this puzzle is for a small child likely to put the pieces into their mouth, I suggest using thinned food coloring to provide color. It can be absorbed quickly and seep into the grain, so a practice piece is recommended.

**10**

Let the paint dry thoroughly. If the recipient is unlikely to put the puzzle into their mouth, once the paint is dry put a light coat of finish on the brontosaur side of the puzzle. This will strengthen the wood and reduce fuzzing produced during the next step.

**11**

Place the brontosaur side down and cut out the puzzle pattern. A new scroll saw blade is recommended to reduce fuzzing. After the pieces are separated, the final coats of finish can be added. Again, if the recipient of the puzzle is likely to put the pieces into their mouth, stick with a non-toxic finish.

# SPOON AND FORK

## Ages 9 to 12

While chopsticks may be the easiest utensils to make, not everyone can figure out how to use them. For these folks a fork and spoon are more suitable.

**Project Pattern**

**Select and cut a 6-inch length of 1-inch thick branch.** Look at the bark. It should be smooth and clean. If there is no bark, be sure the grain is straight and free of imperfections. The branch may be sawn lengthwise or split in half with a hatchet or sturdy pocketknife.

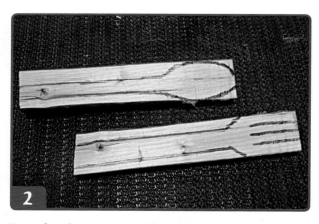

**Transfer the spoon and fork patterns onto the flat faces of the two halves.**

**Starting with the spoon, use the round Microplane to remove the excess wood from the sides of the spoon handle.** When the handle is thinned, round the profile of the bowl.

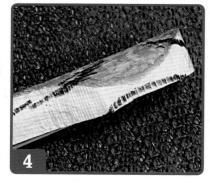

**Turn the spoon on its side and sketch in the bowl and the handle.**

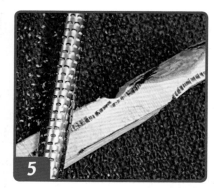

**Starting at the back of the bowl, use the round Microplane to cut in a stop cut at the back of the bowl.** Starting at the spot of the stop cut, thin the handle using long strokes.

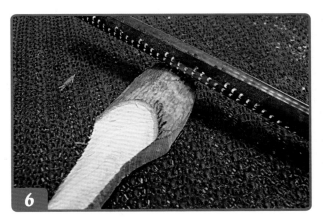

**6**

After the handle is thinned, begin work on the back of the bowl by rounding all of the surfaces. Taper toward the front of the bowl as sketched earlier.

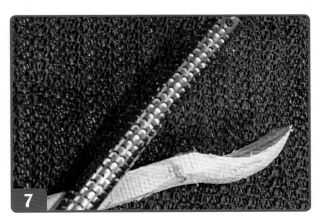

**7**

As in the sketch, use the Microplane to shape the inside of the bowl. When complete, the bowl should have a nice concave shape.

Use the detail sanding stick or sandpaper to sand the bowl smooth. As with the spoon, use the Microplane to thin the handle and shape the end of the fork.

**8**

At this point, you can use a saw to cut the tines, though some might wait until the fork is more completely shaped. Use the Microplane to thin the tines of the fork.

**9**

Use the round sanding stick for a smoother finish. Use the detail stick to smooth the whole fork. Use the detail stick to point the tines.

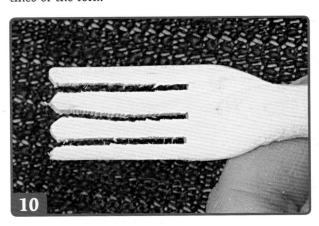

**10**

Be sure to sand between the tines.

**11**

A few drops of mineral oil make a good finish. These implements will need to be re-oiled periodically.

# TOY FISHING ROD AND FISH

## Ages 9 to 12

This easily produced toy can provide amusement for a child while the adults finish preparing and serving the picnic meal.

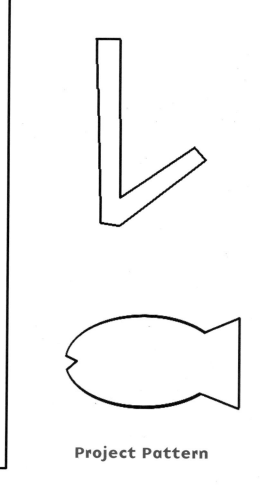

**Project Pattern**

**Select a straight-grained branch about 1 inch in diameter and about 12 inches in length.** With a hatchet or sturdy pocketknife split the piece in half. Select one of the halves and split off the left ⅓ of the stick. Then split off ⅓ from the other side.

**Select and cut a 6-inch length of 1-inch thick branch.** Look at the bark. It should be smooth and clean. If there is no bark, be sure the grain is straight and free of imperfections. The branch may be sawn lengthwise or split in half with a hatchet or sturdy pocketknife.

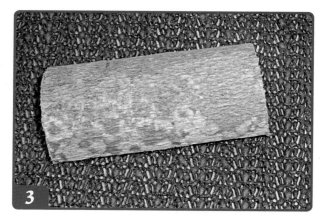

**Retrieve the remaining half of the stick and cut off about 2½ inches.**

34

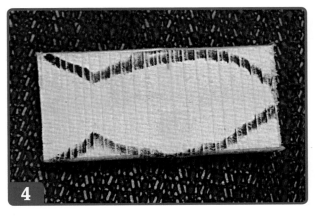

**4**

Transfer the fish pattern onto the flat part of the wood.

**5**

Use the square sanding stick to remove the wood between the tail and the body. Be sure to prepare both sides.

**6**

When the sides are complete, use the flat part of the square sanding stick to narrow the head and mouth area of the fish. Make sure both sides are even. This photo shows the completed stick and fish.

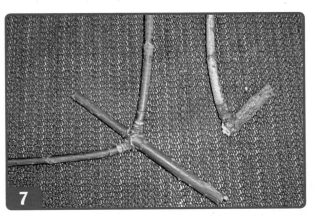

**7**

Find a small stick that has at least one branch attached. This will be used to form our hook. The stick on the left is a good example. Break off the extra wood so it resembles the stick on the right.

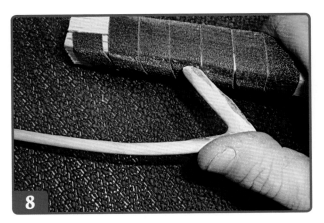

**8**

Sand all the surfaces of the wood and be sure to round the ends so there are no sharp points.

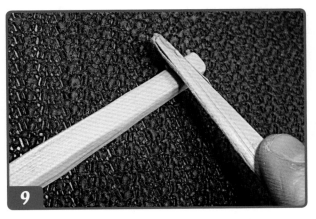

**9**

Use the detail stick to sand a groove about ¼ inch from one end of the stick.

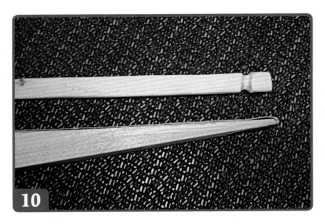

**10**

The groove should be about this wide.

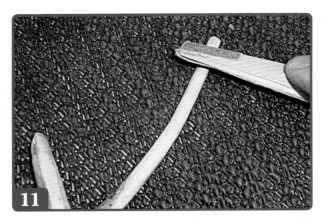

**11**

Make the same groove on the end of the hook.

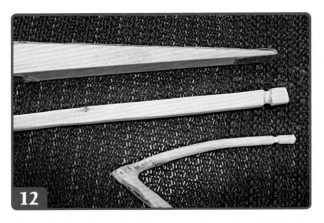

**12**

**Here, the hook and pole are ready to be attached to each other.** Measure a piece of thin cord about 12 inches in length. Tie one end securely to the end of the pole.

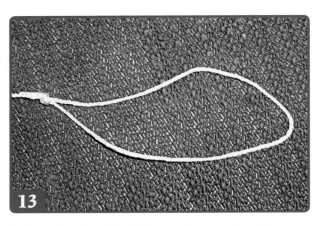

**13**

**Cut another length of the cord approximately a foot long.** Tie the ends in a knot.

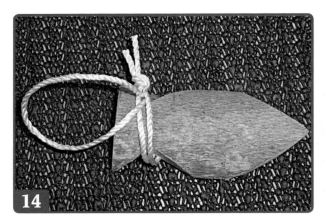

**14**

**Create a captive loop like a lasso and put the loop around the fish tail and pull it taut.** The remaining loop should be stiff enough to stand up somewhat so that it can be hooked with the fishing pole.

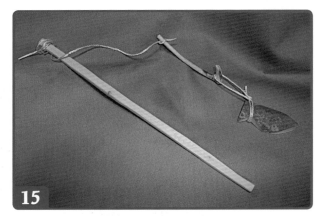

**15**

**Since wood floats, if there is safe water nearby, the little fish can be tossed in and fished out repeatedly, or it can be placed on the ground.** If the student is motivated, the remainder of the wood can be used to make multiple fish.

# WATERMELON KNIFE

## Ages 9 to 12

This project was inspired by a sunny summer afternoon. On a day trip, my wife Joyce pointed out a farm stand full of wonderful produce. Among the fresh fruits we bought was a watermelon. After we had spent a busy afternoon we stopped in a park and decided we couldn't resist the watermelon any longer. I found a sturdy branch to make a tool to cut the fruit.

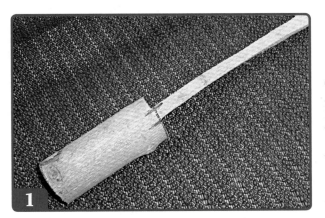

**Choose a sound branch at least 14 inches long.** Mark a 5-inch long handle and then use a saw to make a cut above the handle on both sides. This should leave a ¼-inch wide blade. Split off the wood on either side leaving the blade.

**Use a Microplane or sanding stick to smooth the blade and thin it down toward the side that will be the edge.** When the blade is smoothed, round the tip to a point.

**Project Pattern**

Use the square sanding stick, or the square Microplane, to carve teeth into the edge of the knife.

**We discarded our watermelon knife as soon as it had outlived its immediate purpose,** but if we had decided to add it to our kitchen tools, it would benefit from a coat of edible oil. A knife like this could make an excellent salad knife, as well.

# GEOCACHE TRADE ITEM

## Ages 13 and up

Geocachers are people that search for geocaches using a GPS receiver. When the cache is found, the geocachers make an entry in the cache's logbook, then trade an item in the cache for something they brought. The cache is then returned to its hiding spot.

When we first started geocaching, we rounded up a few smaller carvings, but they were quickly traded out on our first few outings. I came up with something that could quickly be carved out of regular ¼-inch wood.

This project would be best prepared before the outing. Cut out the blanks and bring along the basic tools needed. Select a piece of straight grained stock at least 3 x 2 x ¼ inches.

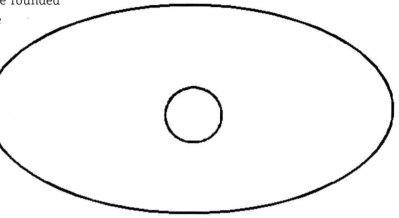

**Project Pattern**

**1**

**Transfer the design to the wood.** Saw the oval shape using a band or scroll saw.

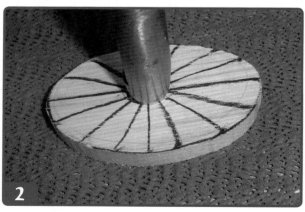

**2**

**Use a ½-inch punch to create a stop cut for the center of the flower.** This could also be accomplished with a v-tool or the bench knife.

**3**

**Use the ⅜-inch v-tool to separate the petals of the flower.** Carve from the outside of the flower in toward the stop cut at the center that was made with the punch. When the task is complete, the flower should resemble this photo.

**To begin shaping the outside of the petals,** make a stop cut at about 45 degrees into the v-tool cut on one side of the v-tool cut.

Do the same on the other side of the v-tool cut and a single chip should pop out. Work your way around the entire flower until all the petals are separated.

When completed, the carving should resemble this photo.

**Use the bench knife to round the center of the flower.** Then use the bench knife to round the petals. This task will change for nearly every petal as each petal is situated in a slightly different direction in relation to the grain. Before starting each petal, take a thin shaving to test the grain direction instead of making a large cut, which might spoil the carving.

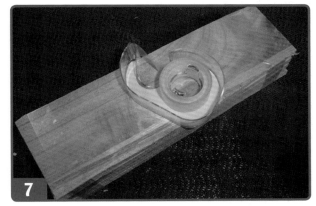

With the prototype done, stack several boards and tape them firmly together.

**Transfer the design to the stack.** Bring the stack to the band saw. A scroll saw will not be effective for this task. Remember to adjust the band saw guide to accommodate the thicker stock. If the band saw guide is too high, the blade will bend during the cutting process and the flowers will not all be the same size.

**Plan the cuts so that the blanks are captive and will not slide around.** Here, as I completed each cut, the waste wood held the rest in place.

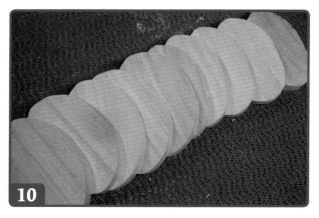

**10**

It took just a few moments to create this stack of blanks.

**11**

**The carving process is the same.** Start by setting in the stop cut for the center of the flowers.

**12**

**Use the v-tool to separate the petals.** Use the bench knife to round the end of the petals, then to round the entire petal as before, keeping in mind that the grain will change direction as you go around.

**13**

**Use a v-tool, toothed stamp, or wood burner to crosshatch the center of the flower.**

**14**

**Glue a tongue depressor to the back of each flower and paint each with a bright yellow.** Lastly, when the paint is dry, attach a packet of daisy seeds to each tongue depressor, using a dot of hot glue.

# Section Three: Music and Noise

*There's something quite magical about wooden musical instruments. Drill a hole and make a few cuts and something is created that can get someone's attention from hundreds of yards away. It's wonderful to make something beautiful, even better to make something beautiful and functional, but the added component of sound can be irresistible.*

*Wood makes interesting percussive noises on its own, but taming and shaping it to form notes is a great deal of fun. Even so, wind instruments created from wood can be painstaking. A basic whistle can be a simple project, but transforming that basic concept into a multi-toned instrument can involve a great deal of trial and error.*

*In general, hardwoods perform better for instruments. Cocobolo and rosewood are among the favorites of percussionists, but they are expensive and difficult for a younger carver to work. Fortunately, pine produces reasonable results.*

# WOODEN CLAPPER

## Ages 4 to 8

Of all the things that make noise, clappers are a percussion instrument that people can't seem to resist testing. A flipping motion of the wrist results in a delightfully satisfying noise that is surprisingly louder than you would expect. In this case, much of the work of creating the instrument is in the preparatory stages and the carver decorates and personalizes the clapper.

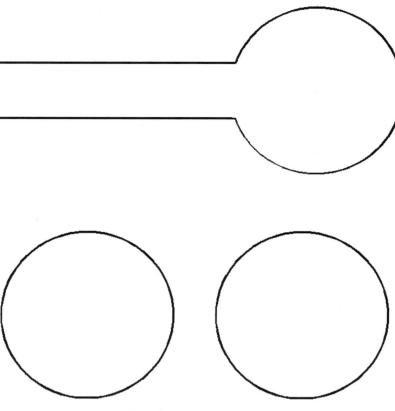

**Project Pattern**

**1**

**Select two pieces of 5 x 8 x ¾-inch thick pine.** The wood should be free of knots, but the straightness of the grain will not make much of a difference in this project. Transfer the pattern onto one piece and scribe two 4-inch circles onto the other one by setting the compass points 2 inches apart.

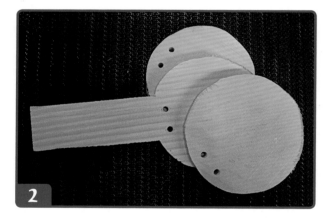

**2**

**Cut out the parts with a band or scroll saw.** Place the three pieces so that the three circles are lined up and the grain is aligned more or less straight. Drill two ¼-inch holes about a half inch apart just about ⅜ of an inch in from the outside of the circle. Sand all surfaces of all parts. When the piece is completed, elastic cord will be strung through these holes to make the clapper function.

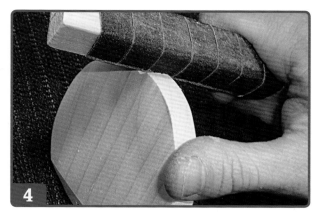

**Have the student take the square sanding stick and sand a 30-degree bevel.** This bevel will be about 2½ inches wide. It should start at the edge of the circle and extend ¼ inch past the drilled holes. Note: Do this on only one side of the piece.

Do this for both of the outside circles, but do not modify the circle with the handle.

**Choose one of the circles and have the carver use the corner of the square sanding stick to remove v-shaped sections around the outside of the circle.** The square Microplane can also be used for this task if it is safe for the carver to use one. When the first outside circle is complete, direct the carver to do the same to the second. This beveled edge will be on the inside of the finished piece. Again, the circle with the handle is not used.

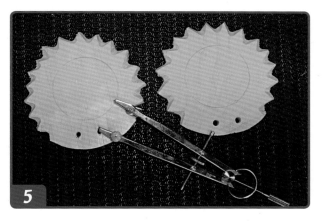

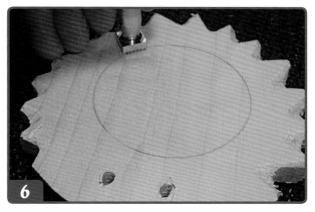

**Setting the points of the compass 1 inch apart, scribe a 2-inch circle on the outside of the two outside circles.** By way of reminder, the outside of the circle is the side without the bevel across the drilled holes.

**Using the square stamping tool, stamp down the area outside the scribed circle, leaving the scribed circle higher than the outside.** When the first circle is done, direct the student to stamp the second one in the same fashion.

**Instruct the carver to make a smiley face in the center of the scribed circle.** To accomplish this, the carver will need a broad flat screwdriver and a flat circular stamp. The simplest way to create such a stamp is to take a large nail, grind off the point, and polish the face. Failing that, grind the point off of a smaller nail, polish the head of the nail, and use the head.

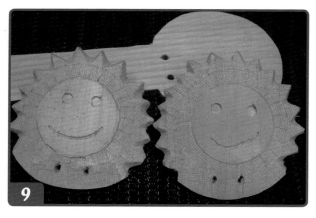

**Assist the student with placing the stamp for the eye and strike the smooth circular stamp once to set in each eye.** Repeat this task on the second circular piece as well. To set in the smile, switch to the flathead screwdriver and show the carver how to set in a smile by setting in a series of short lines in a curved pattern.

**Repeat the step for both circles.** The pieces are now ready to be assembled. If the carver wishes to paint the clapper, perhaps using a sunny yellow color, they should be painted, finished, and dried before the assembly step.

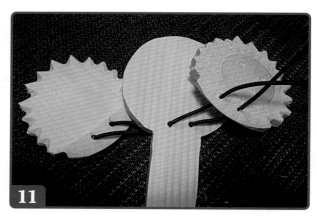

**Take a 1-foot length of elastic cord and thread it through one of the circles so that the ends of the cord are equal in length and rest on the inside.**

**String both ends of the elastic cord through the centerpiece and through the other circle.** Pull the cords taut and tie them with a temporary knot. You will need to adjust the tension of the elastic cord a few times before the clapper has the right amount of action. When this is done, tie a permanent knot and cut any excess cord.

As mentioned above, the piece could be painted or left natural with a light coat of polyurethane to prevent soiling, but those steps should be performed before the final assembly.

# Simple Xylophone

## Ages 4 to 8

This very basic instrument can be carved and assembled quickly. Add more notes or use longer pieces of wood to produce different tones.

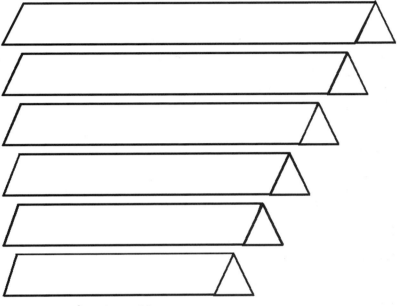

**Project Pattern**

**Prepare a piece of clear hardwood at least ¾ x ¾ by 9 inches long.** For this project, I used walnut as it sands a bit faster than some other hardwoods yet still has a decent tone. Mark one of the ends diagonally from corner to corner.

**If your scroll saw or band saw has a tilting table, you should be able to readily make this cut.** Otherwise, you may need to sand down to produce this shape.

If you can saw one piece, you will have two pieces, triangular in cross section. If you plan your cuts, you should be able to cut six pieces 3, 3 ½, 4, 4 ½-, 5, and 5½ inches long. Cut two pieces of pine ¾ x 3 x 8 inches long. Get the carver started on sanding the walnut pieces smooth.

**3**

While the carver is sanding, get another piece of walnut 6 x ¾ x ¾ inches and transfer the mallet pattern onto the stick.

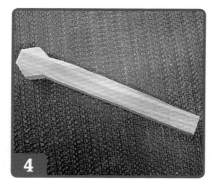

**4**

Cut out the mallet using a scroll or coping saw.

**5**

Arrange the pieces, smallest to largest on the pieces of pine. Space them evenly.

**6**

Mark where each walnut piece is sitting.

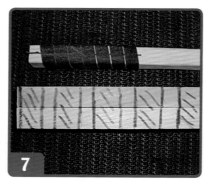

**7**

To make sure the right areas are shaped, mark the wood to be removed with diagonal lines.

**8**

Instruct the carver to use a corner of the square stick to sand in a v-shaped notch into which the walnut pieces will be placed. Keep a consistent depth all the way down.

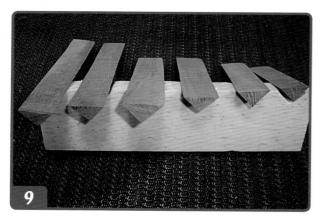

**9**

**Check the walnut pieces for fit.** The pieces need to fit snugly or the sound might be dampened. Encourage the carver to complete both pieces.

**10**

**Dry-fit all the pieces.** Use fine sandpaper to smooth the pine pieces.

**11**

Pour a dot of glue into each of the notches. Fit the walnut pieces into the pine pieces and clamp the assembly together until dry.

**12**

While the glue dries, the carver can work on the mallet. Start by rounding the bottom of the ball end of the mallet where it meets the stick.

**13**

The bottom of the ball is shaped correctly in this photo. Use the same sanding stick to round the stick and reduce its diameter to match the sanding at the bottom of the rounded ball.

**14**

Make sure the carver uses long strokes and works evenly over the entire stick so the handle is straight and smooth. With the stick complete, begin shaping the ball at the end of the stick. When the shaping of the stick is done, sand the entire mallet with fine sandpaper.

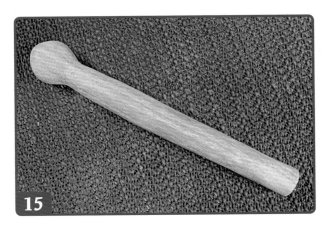

**15**

Here the stick is complete.

**16**

If the glue joint between the walnut and pine is nice and tight, striking the bars with the mallet should produce different tones.

# NOTCHED STICK NOISEMAKER

## Ages 4 to 8

This simple percussion instrument can be created quickly and can easily be customized to create various sounds.

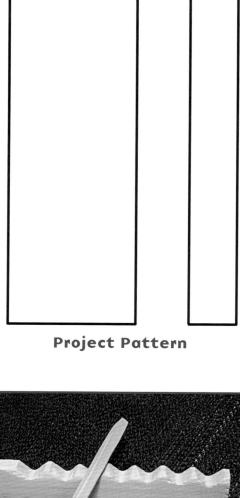

**Project Pattern**

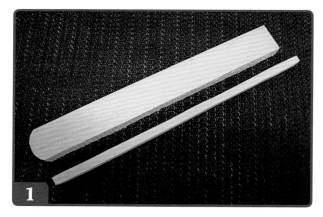

**Select a piece of clear white pine about 8 inches long and at least 3 inches wide.** From this board, lay out one piece ¾ x 2 x 8 inches and another piece ¾ x ¾ x 8 inches.

Cut these two pieces out. Slightly round one end of the ¾ x 2 x 8-inch piece.

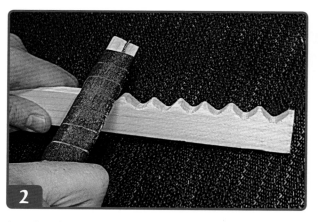

**Starting from the non-rounded end of the ¾ x 2 x 8-inch piece, use the square sanding stick to create evenly spaced notches along the stick.** Leave enough room for a handle. When the notches are complete, sand both the notched stick and the smaller stick.

**Rubbing the smaller stick up and down along the notched stick makes an interesting percussion sound.**

# SIMPLE WHISTLE

## Ages 9 to 12

Whistles can be more art than science, and it might take a few tries to get it right. Prepare a few blocks cut from eastern white pine that are ¾ x ¾ x 5 inches long.

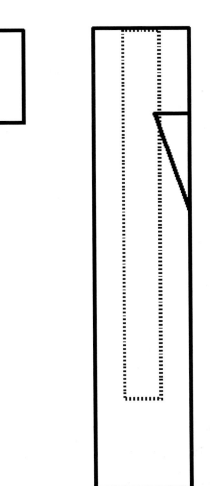

**Project Pattern**

**Drill a ⅜-inch hole 4½ inches deep.** This is best accomplished with the wood clamped to the table of a drill press. Use a carpenter's square to make sure the whistle is perfectly vertical. These holes can be drilled with some careful work using a hand drill, but it will be difficult not to drill out through the side. Be sure that the holes stop before they go through the entire whistle.

**Carve the fipple next.** This will be a piece of pine carved or sanded into a cylinder that fits snugly into the hole drilled into the whistle. It should be just about ⅜ x 1 inches. You could prepare a long fipple and cut pieces off as necessary for each whistle.

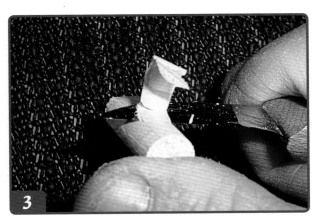

**Pare or sand a flat spot onto the fipple.** The thickness of the wood removed should not be thicker than the back of the bench knife in the photograph.

Lay the fipple on one of the flat parts of the whistle. Mark the whistle at the end of the fipple.

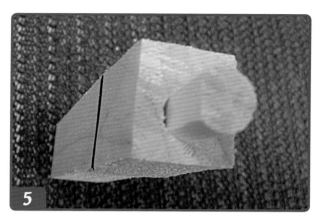

Line up the flat spot with the marked face and press it into place.

The fipple should be flush with the end and a small gap should be visible from the flat of the fipple.

At the mark make a stop cut.

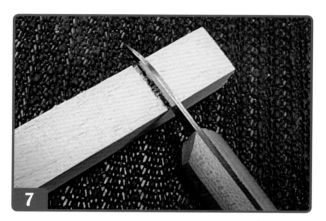

Pare up to the stop cut at about 30 degrees.

Repeat this process until you reach the hole bored earlier.

**10**

**11**

**Because of the angled cuts, the hole that appears should be shaped like half an oval.** This is the moment of truth. Give the whistle a blow and see what happens. Chances are you will get some kind of note if you followed the directions carefully. If not, try shaving a little bit more off the notch or making the flat of the fipple a little deeper. If all else fails, start with one of your back-up whistle blanks. Once you get it right, you'll know and be able to repeat the process.

**Make a few cuts to finish the whistle.** Carve off the corners of the whistle to make an octagon shape. You will need to change directions to accommodate the grain. Be sure to pare off any remaining saw-marks and be careful not to change the shape of the hole.

**12**

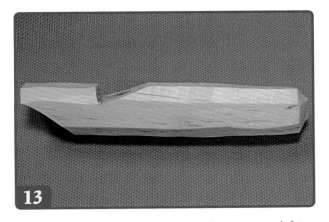

**13**

**To make the whistle more comfortable, undercut the bottom of the mouthpiece.** This will make room for the lower lip. Trim the saw marks off the bottom of the whistle.

**Pleased with successful results, the carver might want to carve up all the practice blanks you made and decorate them with chip-carving or paint.** You could also drill a smaller hole across the bottom to make a necklace. Be careful not to bore into the original hole for the whistle.

# DOUBLE WHISTLE

## Ages 9 to 12

The double whistle can give you two tones. Adding finger holes increases the musical possibilities.

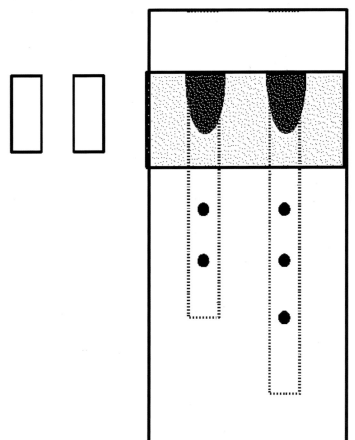

**Project Pattern**

**1**

**Choose a piece of white pine at least 3 x 8 x ¾ inches.** As before, you might want to prepare a backup in case the sound is not satisfactory.

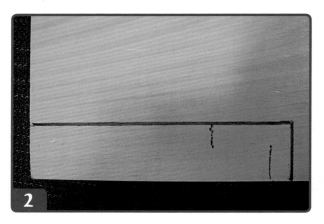

Transfer the pattern to the blank and mark the depths of the holes for the two notes.

**Carve the fipples next.** This will be a piece of pine carved, or sanded, into a cylinder that fits snugly into the hole drilled into the whistle. It should be just about ⅜ x 2 inches. This short dowel will be cut in half to make two 1-inch fipples. You could prepare a longer dowel and cut pieces off as necessary if the first fipples are unsatisfactory.

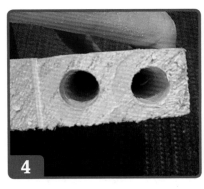

**4**

Drill the two ⅜-inch holes in the whistle, one 5 inches and the other 6 inches deep. This is best accomplished with the wood clamped to the table of a drill press. Use a carpenter's square to make sure the whistle is perfectly plumb.

**5**

Mark a line 1 inch from the end with the drilled holes.

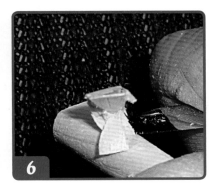

**6**

Pare, or sand, a flat spot onto each of the fipples. The thickness of the wood removed should not be thicker than the back of the bench knife in the photograph.

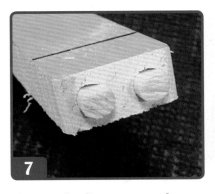

**7**

Line up the flat spots on the fipple with the marked face and press them into place.

**8**

Make a saw cut at the drawn line about ⅓ of the depth of the wood.

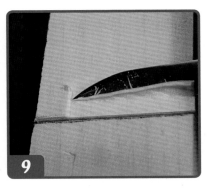

**9**

Pare up to this stop cut until there is about a 30-degree angle. Stop as soon as you reach the hole bored earlier. Start testing the whistle and adjust the fipple or carve the opening slightly larger until you like the sound.

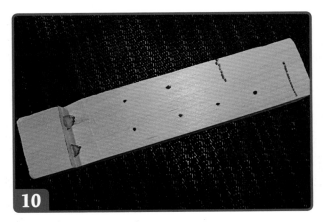

**10**

If you wish to experiment with different tones, mark two finger holes on the shorter whistle and four on the longer.

Drill ⅛-inch holes into the whistle as marked, being careful not to drill out through the other side.

**11**

Under the mouthpiece, draw a curved line as in the photo. Use a bench knife to undercut the bottom of the mouthpiece. This will make room for the lower lip.

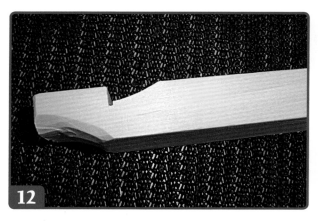

**12**

When complete, the mouthpiece should resemble the photo.

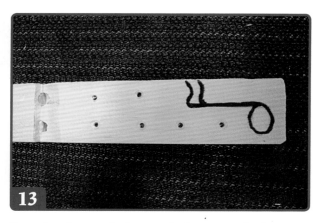

**13**

Transfer the musical note design onto the lower part of the whistle.

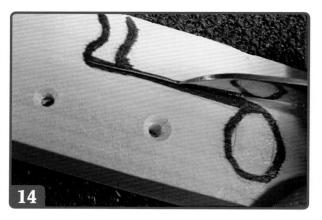

**14**

**A v-tool can be used to incise the design, or as portrayed in the photo, the chip carving technique with the bench knife can be used.** Make a long stop cut down the vertical line of the note. Then make an angled cut starting from the top of the note, parallel with the stop cut.

**15**

**Turn the piece around and make an angled cut in the other direction to release the chips.** Carve the top of the note using the same technique. Finish the musical note by carving the oval shape with the same three cuts.

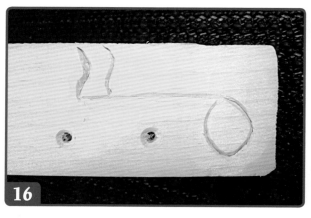

**16**

When completed the carving should resemble this photograph.

You can sand the double whistle smooth or carve the surface with your knife.

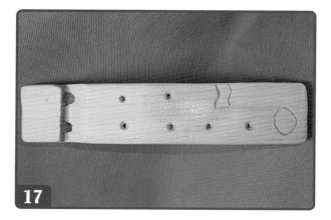

**17**

A light coat of mineral oil will protect this piece.

Section Three: Music and Noise

# Quebecois Spoons

## Ages 9 to 12

This folk instrument is a fond childhood memory. As a very small child at a family event, I remember the smiles from my older relatives when I took two plastic spoons and tried to emulate one of the musicians.

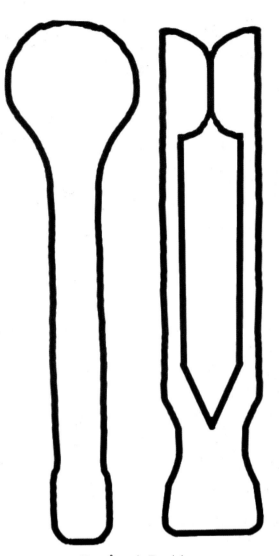

**Project Pattern**

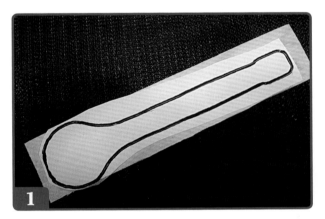

**Select a block of white pine 2 x 2 x 9 inches.** A hardwood might produce a better sound, but would be more difficult to work.

Transfer the top pattern onto the block.

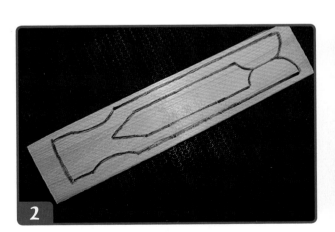

**Transfer the side pattern onto the block, ensuring that the two patterns are lined up.** If the patterns are not lined up, you will not be able to saw out both sides. If you do so, the pieces will not be useful.

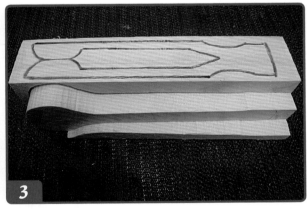

**Saw out the top pattern first.** Try to keep the block as intact as possible so it can be re-assembled and held together with tape to cut the side view.

**4**

**5**

**Here both sides are cut out.** You can see how this technique saves a great deal of work. Mark a circle onto the bowl of each spoon, about ¼ inch from the sides of the bowl. Be sure to do this on both sides.

**With a ⅜-inch #9 gouge, carve from the circle that was drawn earlier into the center of the bowl.** Carve from the other sides to release the chips.

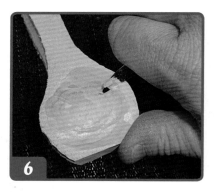

**6**

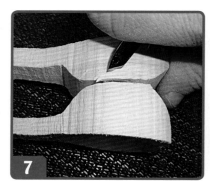

**7**

**8**

**When the bowl is deep enough, use the bench knife to smooth the sides of the bowl.**

**With the insides of the bowls complete, begin to round the outside of the bowls.** Try to work with the grain as much as possible. The walls of the bowl should be at least ¼-inch thick for sturdiness.

**When the side is done, carve down the back of the spoon.**

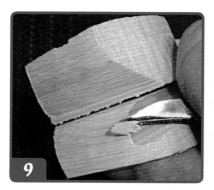

**9**

**10**

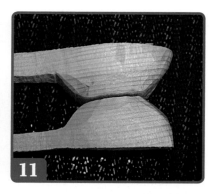

**11**

**Next, carve around the front.** This will be difficult, as it is entirely cross-grain. Try starting at the bottom of the bowl and working toward the edge of the bowl at an angle.

**When that side of the first spoon is done, do the same to the same side of the other spoon.** Most of this work is paring cuts.

**When complete, the side will resemble the photo above.**

**12**

Flip the spoons over and use the same process to shape the other side of the spoons.

**13**

We certainly could sand the handles smooth at this point, but carving off the saw marks leaves an interesting surface. Start by carving from the top of the spoon up the handle at a 45-degree angle to ease the edge. Keep carving around and down the handle, removing the edge and leaving a 45-degree bevel behind.

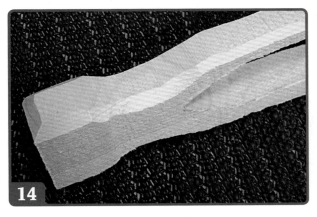

**14**

Flip the spoons over and use the same process to shape the other side of the spoons.

**15**

Next, work on the flat surfaces. Depending on the direction of the grain of your piece, it may be possible to remove a very thin shaving that leaves behind glossy, smooth wood. Carving into the curves is a bit of a challenge. Carve into the curve until you feel the knife start to dive and bite into the wood.

**16**

Switch directions and carve up to the point at which the other cut started to tear.

**17**

The result is a nice clean curve.

**18**

Shave a bit off the thin sides, just enough to remove the saw marks.

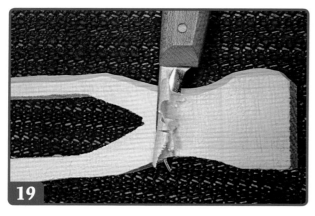

**19**

**The sides of the handle need the same treatment carving from both directions.** First, cut until you feel the tearing. Then reverse and cut from the other direction.

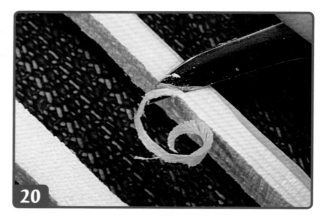

**20**

Bevel the inside of the handles.

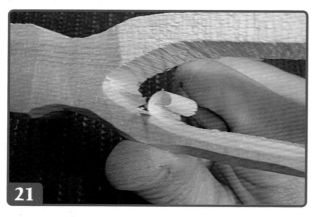

**21**

Make long paring cuts on the insides of the spoon handles.

**22**

Pare down the back of the spoon and inside the handles.

**23**

**Bevel the inside of the spoon handles as the outside was beveled earlier.** Look over the entire spoon for remaining saw marks and carve them off.

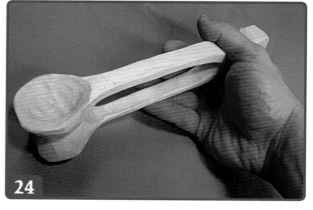

**24**

These spoons will be handled a lot, so finish them with several coats of polyurethane.

# Box Drum

## Ages 13 and up

This box drum takes its inspiration from what is probably the earliest of wooden instruments, the hollow log. The openings in the vine work allow the sound to escape.

Prepare four pieces of eastern white pine that are 5¼ x 9⅜ x ¼ inches and two that are 5¼ x 6 x ¼ inches. You may vary the measurements to fit the wood available, but the pieces must fit together to form a box. Sand the wide surfaces and use a jointer, if available, to square off the sides. A hand plane or careful sanding work is required if no jointer is available. Do not round any corners.

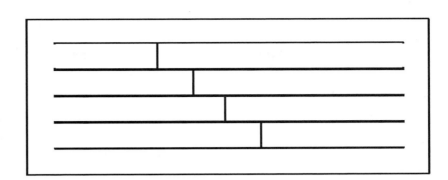

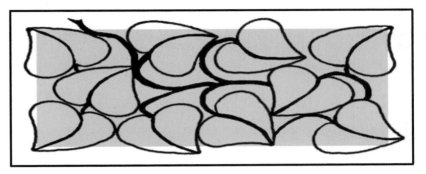

**Project Pattern**

**1**

**Make a copy of the pattern using a copy machine and put the pattern on one of the larger pieces that has the clearest and straightest grain.** Place the copy face down on the board and use a hot, dry iron to heat up the pattern and melt it onto the board.

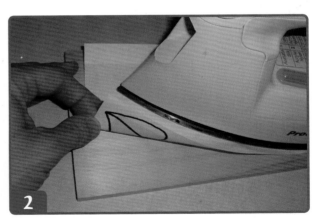

**2**

**Check carefully to see if there is progress.** Depending on the type of toner and the heat of the iron, a great deal of pressure may be required to do this successfully. If your results are less than entirely successful, sketch in the necessary details.

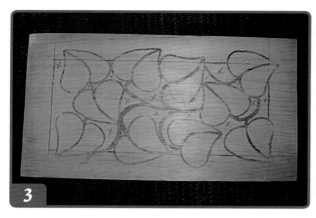

Since there are so many lines in this design, draw small Xs where you will need to make pilot holes to fit the scroll saw blade.

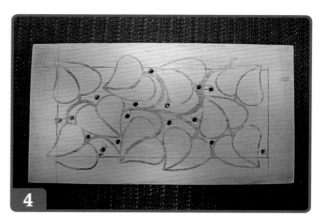

**Drill the pilot holes.** After examining the design more carefully, I elected not to drill some of the pilot holes. These areas will be carved deeply, but not entirely through. This should make the final result less fragile.

**This scroll saw work will be tedious, removing and inserting the scroll saw blade repeatedly.** The thin vines were left wider than the design, again to strengthen the final carving,

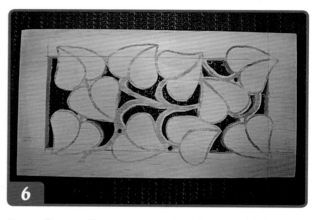

**Here, the scrollwork is completed.** Some of the smaller openings were left and will be carved with the knife.

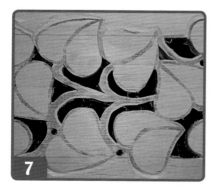

Start with the ⅜-inch v-tool and carve the outlines of the outermost leaves.

Using a ¾-inch-wide #3 gouge, lower the background around the leaves so they are raised higher than the background.

**In the tiniest areas where leaves meet and there is a gap,** draw in six-cut chips.

**10**

The six-cut chips take a stop cut for each of the lines. Use three levering cuts to pop out each of the three chips set up by the stop cuts.

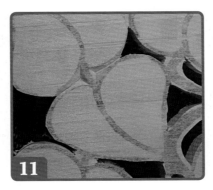

**11**

After the six cuts are completed, an inverted pyramid shape will be visible. Repeat this process for each of the similar areas in the design.

**12**

Using the ⅜-inch v-tool again, carve the centerline of each of the leaves. Take several passes to get a nice, deep line without crumbling the wood. Continue the process for each of the leaves in the design.

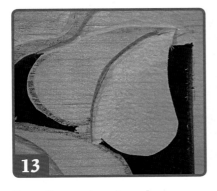

**13**

Once the centers have been set in, use a ¾-inch #3 gouge to deepen the leaves. Begin by removing the corners from the line just made and proceed deeper until there is only one angle, from the edge of the leaf to the lowest part of the center. Here, one lobe of the leaf has been carved.

**14**

Repeat the process for the other lobe of the leaf. The grain changes directions from leaf to leaf so take this into account before you cut. This caution will result in less breakage.

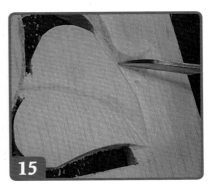

**15**

Use a three-cut to separate the leaf from the adjacent vine. Make a stop cut along the vine first. Then make a stop cut along the leaf. Make a levering cut across the two stop cuts to release the chip.

**16**

In this photo, the depth created by the three-cut is visible.

**17**

Continue the work using the ¾-inch #3 gouge on the leaves, first one lobe, then the other.

**18**

As evident in this photo, each leaf has grain change. Take this into account as you finish setting in all of the leaves.

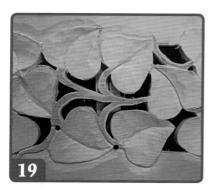

**19**

Here, all of the leaves are completed.

**20**

**The thin vines are the most fragile part of the carving.** Use the bench knife to round each of them. Shave off small amounts rather than taking large chips.

**21**

**The vines are shaped in this photo.** Now, turn the carving over.

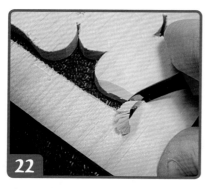

**22**

**An easy way to create the illusion of thinness is to remove wood from the exposed edges around the pierced areas.** Use the bench knife to carve a 45-degree angle on the backs of the leaves and vines. Shave a little at a time rather than taking bold cuts, in order to minimize breakage.

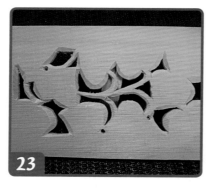

**23**

Here the back of the carving is relieved.

**24**

**With the back relieved, the leaves and vines have the illusion of thinness, but are relatively strong.** The last work is to carve out the two pilot holes.

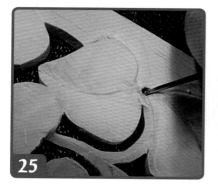

**25**

Make matching angled cuts along the lines around the holes, in this case, along one leaf, the vine, and the other leaf.

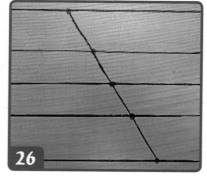

**26**

**Transfer the designs for the drum onto one of the pieces.** Drill pilot holes at the start, end, and intersection of each line.

**27**

Use a scroll or coping saw to cut out the lines.

**28**

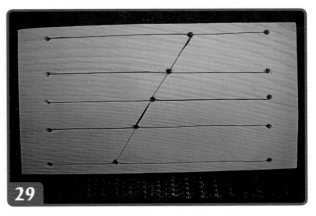

**29**

Each of these tongues of wood must be able to vibrate freely. Sand between them thoroughly, using fine sandpaper.

Here, the drum top is sanded and ready for gluing. Glue and assemble the pieces with the drum on top and the ivy as the front panel. Clamp the box to ensure a good joint.

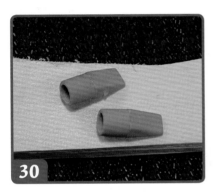

**30**

**31**

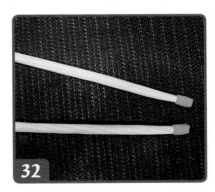

**32**

To begin the drumsticks, start with either two super balls drilled with a ¼-inch hole, or with two pencil erasers.

If using the erasers, cut about ¼ inch off the ends. From another piece of ¼-inch pine, cut two 6-inch lengths, ¼-inch wide, or find dowels of a similar size. Using sandpaper or a Microplane, round the stick.

After shaping, sand the sticks smooth and add the tips.

**33**

**34**

After the box is glued up, you may find that the tongues of the drum do not make a clear ring. To remedy this, insert sandpaper into the scroll sawn lines and sand more until each tongue rings freely when struck.

The completed box drum.

# PAN FLUTE

## *Ages 13 and up*

As a very young child, I was given a pan flute, or syrinx. We were camping at the time and I can remember running through the campground like a young satyr, playing my pipes.

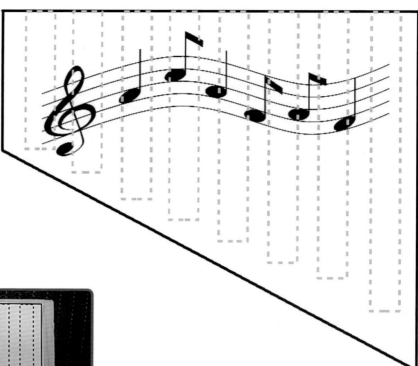

**Project Pattern**

**Select a piece of white pine with very straight and even grain at least 8 x 6 x ¾ inches.** Sand one of the faces smooth and transfer the pattern onto it either by re-drawing, temporary adhesive spray, or your favorite method.

**Mark a centerline across the top of the flute.**

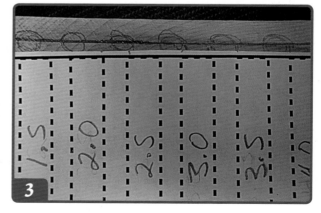

**Using the pattern as a guide, mark where the holes will be drilled and their depths.** In this case, I started at 5 inches and went down at half-inch intervals to 1½ inches.

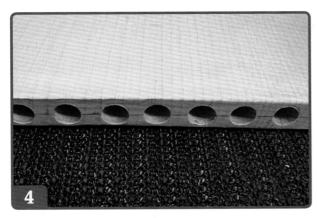

**Drill the ⅜ inch holes as marked.** This is best accomplished with the wood clamped to the table of a drill press. Use a carpenter's square to make sure the board is perfectly vertical. These holes can be drilled with some careful work with a hand drill, but it will be difficult not to drill out through the side. Be sure that the holes stop before they go through the entire piece. After the holes are drilled, take the piece to the band saw and cut out the shape. If the piece were cut out earlier, it would be very difficult to clamp it for drilling.

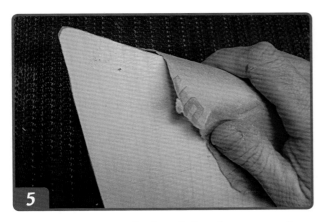

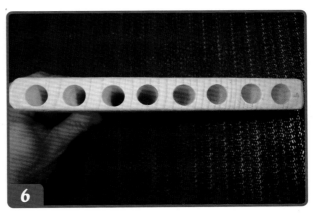

This piece will spend a lot of time in someone's hands and parts of it will be in contact with someone's lips, so sand it well. After sanding, wipe it down with a very slightly damp paper towel to remove the dust. Wrap a piece of fine sandpaper around a pencil and clean out the holes.

Gently tap the panpipe upside down to empty any sawdust or drill shavings.

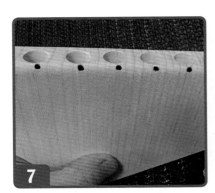

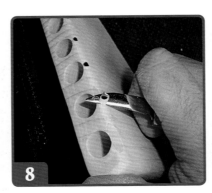

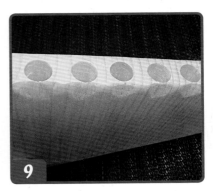

Mark the back of each hole with a small dot.

Remove some wood from behind each hole, like in the scalloped patterns used in the earlier projects. Using a pencil as a sanding stick again, sand each of the scalloped depressions.

This scalloped pattern serves two purposes, to allow the person to position closer to the hole and so that the person can feel when they are changing notes.

If you have not yet applied the pattern of notes, do so now, or touch up your re-drawing.

**Make sure your v-tool is sharpened and buffed.** Moving from right to left, carve each of the long, curved lines first. If you maintain a consistent depth, the line should come up in one long chip.

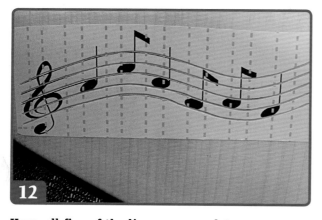

Here, all five of the lines are complete.

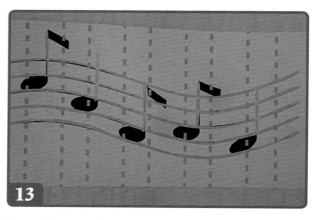

**Proceed to carving the vertical lines for each of the notes.** A sharp tool will prevent tearout when the vertical lines intersect the horizontal ones. In this photograph, the vertical lines of the notes are complete.

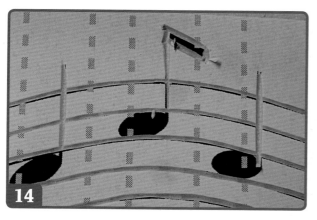

**Next, carve in the flag part of the notes.** Two lines will serve to represent these. Carve from the end of the lines into the vertical part of the note. The second line should end at the tip. Then carve a third line connecting the two lines. Here is one of the notes with the top completed.

**The G-clef requires many turns.** Do not bear down through the curves. Several passes are better than ripping the wood.

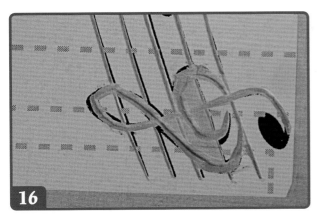

**16**

**The G-Clef is made of a single line.** Start at the bottom and follow it throughout the character.

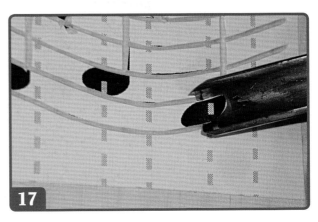

**17**

**Use either a ¼ #9 or #11 gouge to carve in the bottom of the notes.** Carve from the end of the oval to the center and stop. Turn the piece around and carve to the center from the other side of the oval.

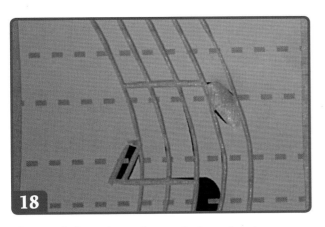

**18**

**The result is a nice, crisp oval-shaped note.**

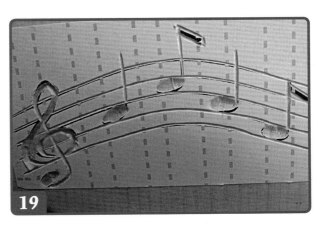

**19**

**Proceed carving the rest of the notes.**

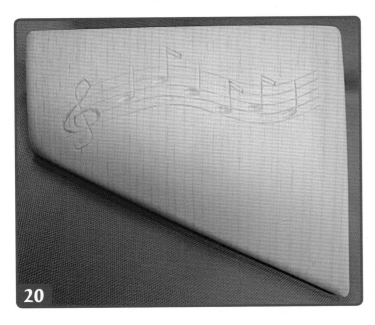

**20**

**When the notes are carved, remove any remaining pattern or drawing marks, sand lightly and finish.** As the piece will be in contact with someone's mouth frequently, a light coat of mineral oil will make a good finish.

# SECTION FOUR: GIFTS

*In the introduction, I discussed the idea of breaking the cycle of consumerism and reviving a culture of "make" and "do." Gift giving is an excellent place to start.*

*It's an old saw that people appreciate a handmade gift more than a store-bought one, but sometimes carvers don't take their work seriously enough. As creative people, we can produce unique gifts whose real dollar values are much higher than we'd likely be able to pay for gifts. Taking the money you would budget for a gift and investing it in raw materials with care and attentive work will pay off.*

*Another benefit of the handmade gift is customization. Incorporating techniques demonstrated in this section, as well as elsewhere in the book, the carver will be able to create a one-of-a-kind gift whose value simply can't be measured in dollars.*

# BASEBALL AWARD

## Ages 4 to 8

This baseball bat design can be lengthened or shortened as desired for the particular name.

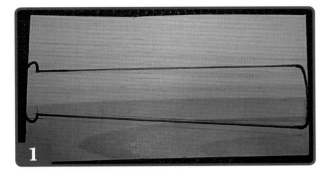

**Choose clear straight grained ¼ inch wood measuring at least 3 x 10 x ¼ inches.** Transfer the design onto the wood.

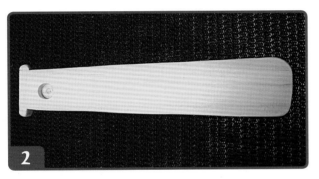

**Cut out the outline with a band or scroll saw, sand all surfaces smooth, and drill a shallow hanging hole in the back of the piece.**

**Project Pattern**

**Draw some guide lines on the bat to help lay out the lettering.** Draw guides ¼ inch in from the sides. As far as the guides for the individual letters, that will be determined by how many letters are required. If there are many letters, consider re-drawing the pattern for a longer bat.

**Draw the letters onto the bat.** Here, I chose to stamp inside the letters, but an older child would be able to stamp the outside, raising the letters. Continue the stamping process for all the letters. Be sure to hit the stamp with even strokes so the stamps are the same depth. The emphasis is on making an impression in the wood, not tearing it.

**When the stamping is done, a light coat of stain will bring out the letters.** Finish with a coat of matte polyurethane spray.

# FOOTBALL PLAQUE

## Ages 4 to 8

My oldest son Robert played a season of Pop Warner football and was nominated most improved by his teammates. We looked for an activity for him during the off season and were introduced to Grandmaster Roger Rodriguez who had a Taekwondo studio across the street from the practice field. During our first conversation, I realized what a great instructor he was and we've been studying with him ever since.

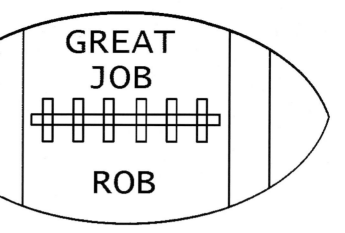

**Project Pattern**

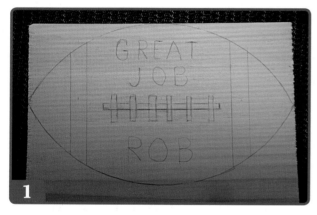

**Select and sand smooth a piece of pine 8 x 6 x ¼ inches and transfer the design to it.** Drawing guidelines will greatly help with laying out the lettering.

**Cut out the football based on the pattern.** Drill a shallow hole in the back of the football, for hanging.

**Using the round sanding stick, round over all the edges.** Re-draw any lines removed during the sanding process.

**Use a flathead screwdriver to stamp in the straight lines of all the letters.** To manage the curves, use a narrower, flathead screwdriver. If the screwdriver is still too wide for the curve, try stamping in just one corner and work your way around the curve.

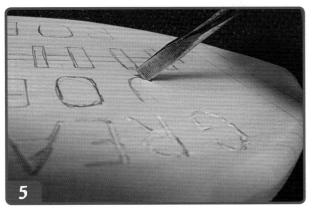

**5**

Be careful to maintain consistent depth for every part of each letter.

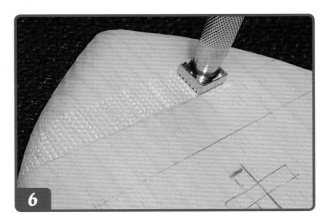

**6**

Use the large square stamp to texture the end of the football. Start by stamping down along the outside edge of the stripe.

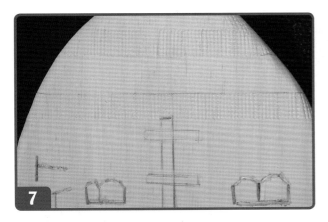

**7**

Do the same along the inside of the stripe. Be sure to do both stripes on the sides of the football.

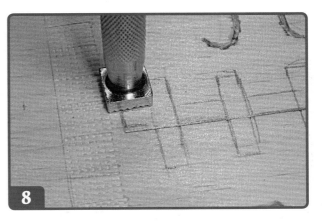

**8**

Begin raising the laces by stamping into the corners of each lace. With the laces raised, now work over all the other surfaces of the football with the square stamp.

**9**

Remember to turn the stamp frequently and cover the surface evenly.

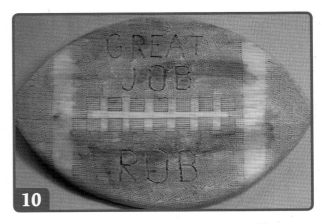

**10**

The finished carving can be completed with a light staining or could easily be painted. If it is desired to paint the inside of the letters a contrasting color, stamp the letters, fill with paint, allow it to dry, sand the excess paint, redraw the pattern and proceed with the rest of the process.

## Ages 4 to 8

If you love Nanna's cookies, a little bribe couldn't hurt to encourage her to bake up a batch.

**NANNA'S KITCHEN**

### Project Pattern

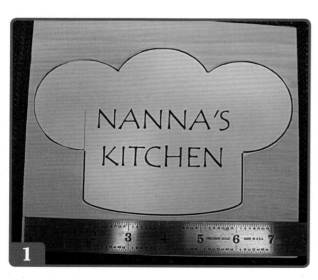

**1**

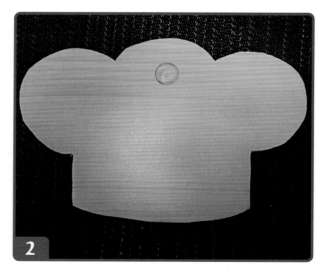

**2**

**Chose a well-sanded piece of 8 x 6 x ¾-inch pine for this kitchen sign and transfer the pattern.** Cut the profile out using a band or scroll saw.

**Drill a shallow hole in the back so that the carving may be hung when completed.**

**3**

Start with the square sanding stick and deepen the "V" areas at the top of the hat. Use the flat sides of this sanding stick to round all the rest of the edges of the hat.

**4**

When shaped, the hat should resemble the photo above. Re-draw any lines that were sanded off.

**5**

The primary tool here will be a wide, flathead screwdriver. Instruct the student to stamp the lines of the letter to a consistent depth.

**6**

Continue onto the other letters in the first line. The curves of the "S" pose a problem for the flathead screwdriver. Press the corner of the screwdriver into the lines of the "S," then turn the screwdriver slightly farther around the curve and repeat. Once the first line is complete, proceed to the second. Use the same technique to stamp in the letters.

**7**

Use the same technique on the letter "C" as on the letter "S" earlier. Maintain a consistent depth, especially with the curved letters.

**8**

When the letters are complete, the hat should resemble the one in the photo. A couple of coats of satin polyurethane will protect it from kitchen grease and allow it to be wiped down occasionally.

# DESK SET

## Ages 9 to 12

What did we do before yellow stickies? This project is designed for a 3 x 3 pad, but could easily be changed to accommodate any size.

**Project Pattern**

**Start with a 3 x 3 yellow sticky pad and a piece of eastern white pine 4 x 5 x ¾ inches.** Center the pad of stickies on the lower part of the board and trace its dimensions onto the board.

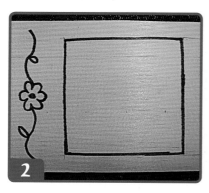

**Transfer the pattern onto the wood using the tracing to help orient the area to be cut out for the pad.**

**Drill a ¼ inch hole for the penholder.** Use your largest drill bit to rout out as much of the wood as possible in the hole to hold the pad. Use a Forstner, or brad point bit, so the holes are as shallow as possible. A drill press is the best tool for this step.

**Use a ¾-inch-wide #3 gouge and make stop cuts just inside the line drawn for the pad.** Continue to work around the inside of the area that will hold the pad. Carve up to the stop cuts.

**5**

**Smooth the bottom of the area with the #3 gouge.** The bottom does not need to be perfectly smooth. However, there should be no bumps that would prevent the pad from lying flat.

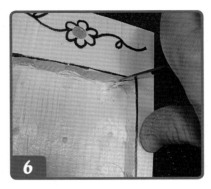

**6**

**Carve a stop cut up to the corner with the knife blade.** Then make another stop cut, releasing the chip and freeing up the corner.

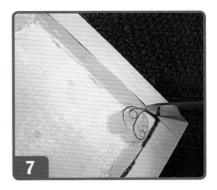

**7**

**Shave the sides square with the bench knife.**

**8**

**Try fitting the pad into the area carved for it.** Where the pad sticks, use the knife to shave down the sides until the pad fits snugly.

**9**

**Use the "V" tool to carve the ornament at the top.** Starting from one of the ends, carve into the center. Next, carve the other vine from the outside toward the center.

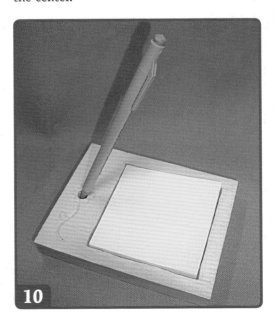

**10**

**Carve the lines of the leaves toward the vine.** Lastly, carve the petals with the "V" tool. Here is the completed pad holder.

# HOLIDAY ORNAMENT

## Ages 13 and up

Several of our family members are in the service and although they are always on our minds, not having them around at the holidays can be especially poignant. This project serves to remind us of their service to our country.

**1**

**Select a piece of clear white pine at least 5 x 4 x ¼ inches and transfer the pattern onto the wood.**

**Project Pattern**

**2**

**Drill a ¼-inch hole between the back of the waist and the rifle to allow that waste to be removed.** Scroll saw the outline and then the interior area between the soldier and the gun.

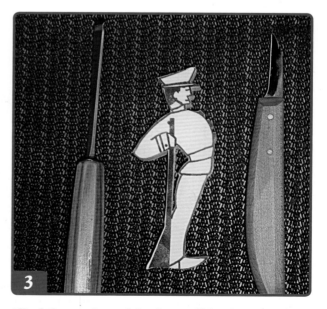

**3**

**All of the work on this piece will be done with the v-tool and the knife.** The soldier could be carved with just the knife, but using the ⅜ inch v-tool will make the work somewhat easier.

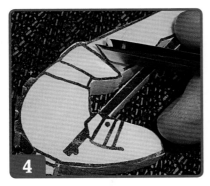

**4**

Starting with the v-tool, cut in most of the lines defined on the pattern, starting with the line defining the separation between the pants and the bottom of the tunic.

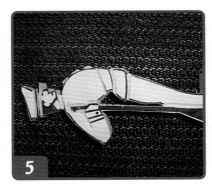

**5**

Here, the v-tool cuts on the pattern side are complete.

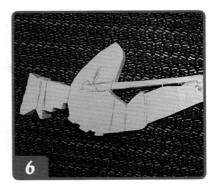

**6**

Once the lines on the pattern side are complete, turn the soldier over and transfer the pattern in reverse to the other side. Make the same v-tool cuts on this side.

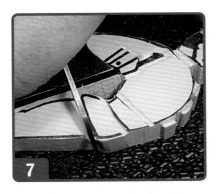

**7**

Most of the next steps involve the same two or three cuts. Start with a stop cut on the edge of the carving, right in the center of the line left by v-tool. Make this cut at a 45-degree angle into the edge of the wood.

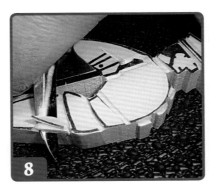

**8**

Pare up the leg to the stop cut at the bottom of the tunic.

**9**

Reverse the blade and pare down from the tunic to the bottom of the pant leg. Repeat the same series of cuts on the reverse. Start with the stop cut under the tunic.

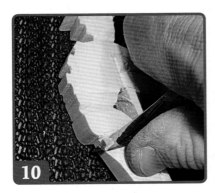

**10**

Pare up to the stop cut. Then again reverse the knife and pare from the tunic down to the bottom of the pants.

**11**

A view from the bottom of the shoe up the pant leg shows the leg shaped with bold cuts.

**12**

Make a stop cut and a small paring cut up to the tunic on the flat of the edge of the soldier.

**13** Make a thin paring cut down the front of the pants from the tunic to the bottom of the leg, in order to remove the saw marks.

**14** The shoe is entirely cross-grained and therefore is quite fragile. Make gentle paring cuts up from the shoe to the bottom of the pants.

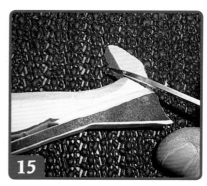

**15** Trim the edge of the pants with a stop cut.

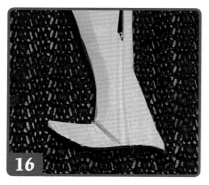

**16** The result of the work on the shoe is shown in this photo.

**17** Begin the back of the leg with a stop cut similar to that on the front of the pants leg.

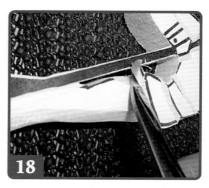

**18** Use the same paring cuts to work the front of the pants. Carve up to the bottom of the tunic. Make a stop cut where the rifle meets the lower part of the leg.

**19** Pare down the leg to this stop cut.

**20** Make another stop cut to define the bottom of the tunic.

**21** Pare up to this stop cut, being sure to remove any pattern remnant still attached.

**22**

On the front edge of the soldier, draw lines approximately ¼ inch apart to define the width of the buttons. Using the v-tool, turned away from the button, carve away the waste wood.

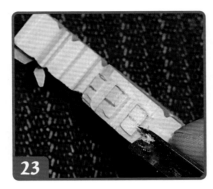

**23**

Once one side is ready, carve away the waste wood from the other side of the buttons.

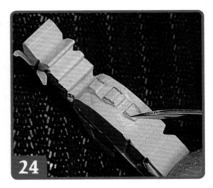

**24**

Round off the buttons by cutting a small amount of wood from each of the corners of the buttons.

**25**

Now that the buttons are complete, return to work on the tunic. Make a paring cut up the tunic to the belt.

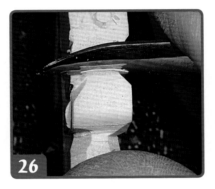

**26**

Make a stop cut on the front edge of the carving where the tunic meets the belt. Pare up to that stop cut to begin shaping the front of the tunic. Starting at the bottom of the tunic, pare up to the belt removing the corner at about a 45-degree angle.

**27**

Be sure to follow these steps for both sides of the carving.

**28**

Make a paring cut from the bottom of the tunic up to the belt on the flat side of the soldier. A paring cut from the bottom of the back of the tunic up to the belt finishes the shaping work on this side.

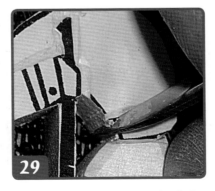

**29**

Make a paring cut from the belt to the tunic where it blouses out above the tightness of the belt. Pare down from the armpit area to the previous cut.

**30**

On the front of the tunic, make another paring cut at a 45-degree angle to the edge. Then pare down to that cut from the tunic to the top of the belt.

**31**

Make the same two cuts on the front of the carving. After the second cut, be sure to carve the reverse side.

**32**

Pare the corner off the front of the belt.

**33**

Then pare the corner off the back of the belt.

**34**

Pare up the tunic from the belt to the neck at a 45-degree angle.

**35**

Make a paring cut up to the v-tool mark to separate the shoulder from the neck.

**36**

Pare off the corner from the elbow up to the shoulder.

**37**

Then pare off the saw marks from the top of the arm. Make a light stop cut at the waist.

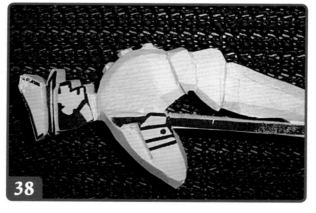

**38**

Depending on the grain of the wood, pare down to the belt or up to the neck to remove any pattern remaining on the tunic. If you have not done so earlier, use the v-tool to cut in the stripe, the cuff and the hand.

Make a 45-degree stop cut at the stripe. Carve off the corner of the lower arm. Then use the same cuts on the reverse side.

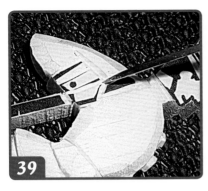

**39**

**A long three-cut will be used to shape the crook of the arm.** Make a stop cut at a 45-degree angle behind the rifle barrel.

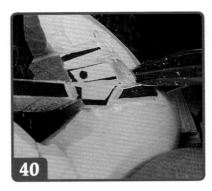

**40**

**Pare up from the elbow along the upper arm to that stop cut at a 45-degree angle.** Make an angled stop cut from the armpit to the elbow, and a chip should be released.

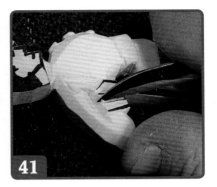

**41**

**Above the stripe, cuff, and hand, use two angled cuts on the corners that will widen the ends of the v-tool cuts.** Proceed first with one angled cut. The second angled cut meets the first and the chip is released.

**42**

**Continue this technique around the cuff and hand on both sides of the soldier.**

**43**

**After the cuffs on both sides are complete, begin to shape the rifle barrel using long paring cuts.** If the wood starts to tear as you begin the cut, reverse the direction you are paring.

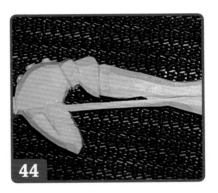

**44**

**Pare up from the bottom of the rifle to the barrel.** Smooth and round the barrel on both sides, being sure to leave enough wood so that the barrel is not too fragile.

**45**

**To define the chin, hairline, and neck, use a three-cut.** First make a stop cut along the jaw line.

**46**

**The next stop cut goes along the hairline.** The last levering cut is up from the neck to the hairline.

**47**

**Separate the hat from the hairline with a stop cut.** Then pare up the hair to the hat to round off that corner of the head.

**Pare up the back of the head to the hat.** Then make a stop cut to release the chips. Make the stop cut and paring cut on the corner of the reverse side.

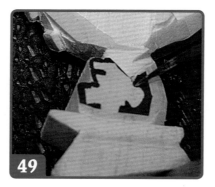

**Raise the earlobe up with another three-cut.** First make a stop cut along the earlobe. Make a second stop cut with the knife tip along the jaw and then make a levering cut to remove the chip. Use three more cuts to release the top of the ear. Begin by cutting along the ear and then along the hairline.

**Carve toward the ear to release the chip.** Use the v-tool lightly to round the back of the ear and connect the previous work.

**Pare away the wood around the ear so the hair is lower than the ear.**

**This photos shows the final shape of the ear.** Now carve the ear on the other side.

**Make a stop cut at the top of the face under the brim of the hat.** Pare from the nose up to the stop cut under the brim.

**Make a stop cut for the eye.** Start at the bridge of the nose and angle back toward the ear. This stop cut should be about ¼ inch long.

Make a very steep paring cut up to the stop cut. This will create a dark shadow that will represent the eye.

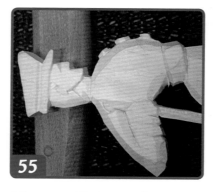

**After one side is complete, do the reverse side.**

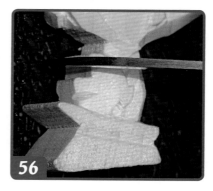

**Use the same technique for the mouth.** Add a stop cut to the corner of the mouth area. Make a steep levering cut up into the stop cut.

**57**

Repeat the technique across the front of the face and on the reverse side to complete the mouth.

**58**

**Shave the saw marks off the top of the hat.** Mark the oval shape of the hat. Pare off the corners of the hat. Be sure to pare all four corners.

**59**

**Make a paring cut down to the original v-tool cuts from the beginning of the carving.** There should be about a 45-degree angle.

Make a stop cut to release the chips. Do the same around the brim area, paring from the brim to the hat. Then pare from the hat to the brim.

**60**

**The sides of the hat receive the same treatment.** Be sure that the angles are consistent and that both sides are carved.

**61**

**The photo here shows the completed hat.**

*(right)* **A coat of polyurethane would finish this nicely, but holiday ornaments should be brightly painted.** If a loved one is a service member or a first responder, the uniform could be painted to resemble theirs. When finished, screw a small eyehook into the top of the hat for hanging.

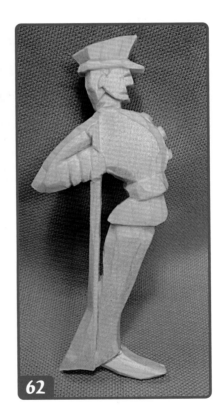

**62**

# SECTION FIVE: WOODCUTS AND ENGRAVING

*It seems a bit strange to extol the virtues of what might be considered a primitive technology while I type into a word processor on a portable computer that is wirelessly connected to a global network. Woodcuts and engravings were among the first methods that humans used to reproduce words and images for mass consumption.*

*Just as the creation by hand of a woodcarving is more satisfying than buying a similar item, the creation of an elegant print can produce a similar satisfaction. Printing from wood is a bit of a process, and certainly you'll find yourself with ink on your fingers and other unanticipated places. The woodcut is a functional work of art that creates art itself.*

*The following projects assume a single ink color printing on paper, but the carver need not limit himself in this fashion. By breaking the components of the design across several blocks, the carver/engraver can create full-color prints. Using fabric paints, the carver/woodcut artist can create unique fashions for himself or to give as gifts.*

*There are several methods of printing. With the smaller projects, a fresh inkpad is probably sufficient. Without an ink pad, using a brush and acrylic paint will work. For the larger projects, the carver will want washable printer's ink, a brayer, and a flat glass or stone surface to roll the ink onto the brayer. These items are available at many craft stores.*

# NAME STAMP

## *Ages 4 to 8*

This name stamp will be
a favorite method to sign
drawings, especially for
the youngest carvers still
struggling with forming
their letters correctly.

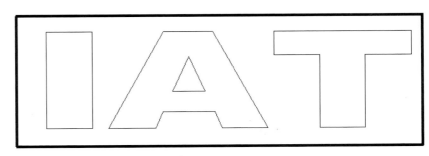

**Project Pattern**

**Choose some straight-grained pine or basswood
that will fit your stamp pad.** Mark off a ¼-inch
border at the top and bottom of the piece.

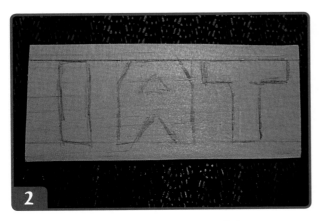

**2**

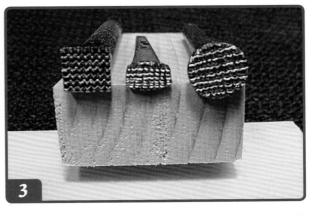

**3**

**Sketch or transfer a mirror image of the name
onto the wood.** If you use a word processing program
to print the name, some printers have a special
setting for t-shirt transfers. This setting will take the
text you type and make a mirror image for you to use
for this step. If you use a word processor, stick with
a big blocky font to make the task easier for the
carver. The tails on some letters, called serifs, will
be fragile and potentially difficult for many younger
carvers to reproduce.

Alternatively, use the block to trace a square on
a piece of paper. Either have the carver write his
or her name or draw the name in some fashion
on the paper, using a very soft leaded pencil.

To transfer the pattern, place it face down on
the block and rub the pattern with the back of
the spoon. If you rub with sufficient pressure, the
pattern will be reversed and transferred to the block.

It is likely however, that the design will be faint
and will need re-drawing.

**To complete this project will likely require several
different punches, depending on the letter style
and the letters in the carver's name.**

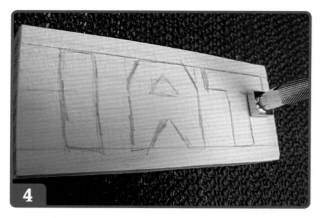

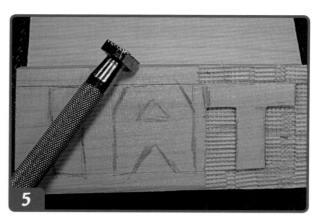

The "T" lends itself to the square stamp, so here I start in the corners of the top of the "T" and work my way around the letter.

Once the letter is completely raised, add an extra strike to the corners to lower them so they are less likely to appear when the stamp is used.

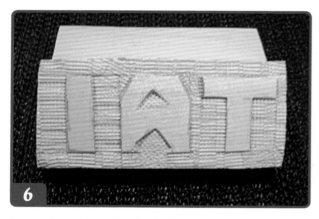

Proceed to lower the background around the letters as with the first letter, using the different stamps to fit the letter shapes. Remember to keep a consistent depth and to lower the outside corners of the block slightly more than the rest.

A well-made stamp will leave a crisp impression, with minimal or no background from the wood around the letters.

# TIC TAC TOE GAME STAMPS

## Ages 4 to 8

While tic-tac-toe may seem a little old-fashioned for today's young carvers, creating the stamps themselves will add novelty to the game.

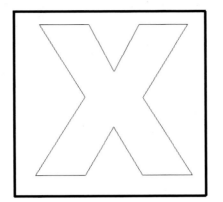

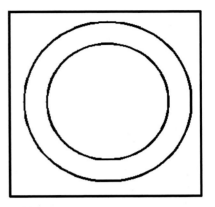

**Project Pattern**

**From a clear piece of ¼-inch pine cut two 2 x 2 inch squares.** Sand all surfaces to a very smooth finish.

**Transfer the drawings onto each of the pieces.**

**For the X pieces, use the toothed, square-shaped stamp.** Place the stamp into one of the corners of the X. Stamp here and work your way along the legs of the X and out to the edge. Repeat for all four sides.

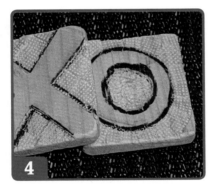

**The square stamp can be used to stamp the 0, but a round stamp will be easier to use.**

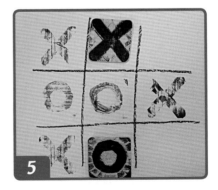

**Once the stamping is completed, they can immediately be tested using an inkpad.** Draw the hash marks for a game of tic-tac-toe and enjoy a game with the carver.

# GIFT TAG STAMP

## Ages 4 to 8

Although this design is simplistic, it should not limit the creativity of the artist to embellish it with appropriate designs.

**1**

Select a piece of ¼-inch thick pine that is well sanded and has a 2 x 3-inch area that is clear and free of defects.

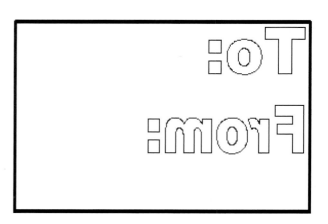

**Project Pattern**

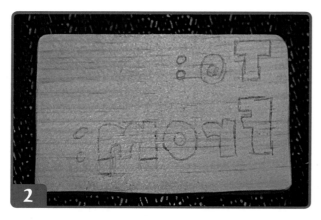

**2**

**Transfer the pattern to the wood or sketch freehand.** Depending on the carver's motor skill development, you could change the size of the stamp and lettering. Larger stamp and letters would be easier for a younger carver.

**3**

**Use a smooth-faced stamp to lower the areas around the letters.** Place the stamp directly against the pencil lines and strike. Be sure to maintain even depths and not to damage the letter shapes. Repeat the process around the outside of each letter. Use a smaller stamp or nail for the inside of the letter "0."

**4**

Once the letters are raised, used a toothed stamp to lower the background.

**5**

Now the letters clearly stand out.

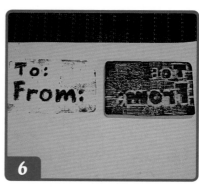

**6**

**Press the stamp onto an inkpad and test it out on paper.** With the basic concepts understood, other stamps can be created using designs that fit the occasion or gift. Several stamps could be combined with different colored inkpads to create interesting effects.

# CHIP-CARVED WOODCUT

## Ages 9 to 12

When I was in Korea, our group visited several museums and I was quite taken with the elegant simplicity of the ink drawings. This crane design evolved out of some sketches I made while in Jeon-ju.

 **1**

**Select a piece of straight-grained wood at least ¾ x 8 x 6 inches.** Pick the better of the two sides and sand it smooth using progressively finer grits of sandpaper.

**Project Pattern**

**2**

Transfer the design to the wood.

**3**

**Most of the lines on this carving will use the same technique.** Carve a stop cut from one end of the line to the other.

**4**

Make an angled cut along the same line.

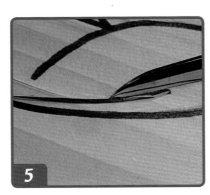

**5**

**Turn the carving around and make another long angled cut along the same line.** The chips will be released as you cut.

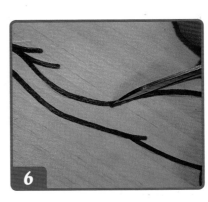

**6**

**The next line to cut is at the back of the neck.** Make a stop cut along the entire length of the line.

**7**

**Make the first angled cut along the line, turn the carving around and make the second.** As you carve the second, the chip will be released.

**8**

**The next line starts at the beak, extends around the head and down to the previous line.** Start the stop cut at the beak.

As you make the angled cut down the back, be aware that the grain is straight and the knife may not want to follow the curve. The third cut releases the chip as before.

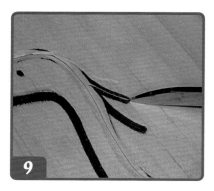

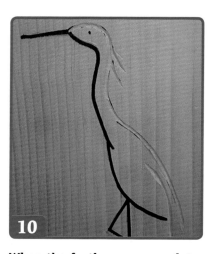

**9**

**Next, carve the raised feathers at the back of the neck.** After the stop cut, make two angled cuts for each of the feathers.

**10**

**When the feathers are complete, the piece should resemble the photo.**

**11**

**Next is the line around the belly.** Make the stop cut, then make the angled cut. Turn the piece around to make the third cut and release the chip.

The next line to cut is the front of the neck. Make the stop cut down the line.

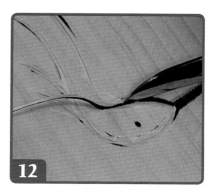

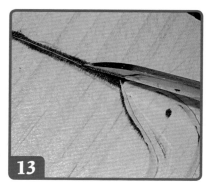

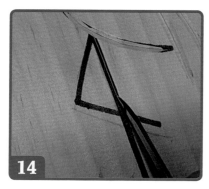

**12**

**Make the two angled cuts to finish carving the line.**

**13**

**To carve the beak, make the stop cut, starting at the tip and cutting back toward the head.** As the beak goes across the grain, the chip may come up in several pieces. Turn the piece and complete the beak.

**14**

**Carve the straight leg first.** The second angled cut will release a long chip.

**15**

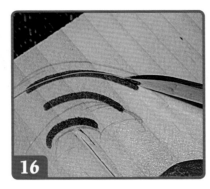

**16**

**17**

**Cut in the upper part of the bent leg.** When cutting in the lower part of the leg, be sure the knife is sharp; if not, the wood from the other leg may crumble.

Make the first levering cut. Then turn the wood around to make another levering cut and finish the leg.

**The ripples are next.** Make the stop cuts, and the levering cut, in one direction.

**The second levering cut releases the chip.** Continue, using the same process for the other ripples.

**18**

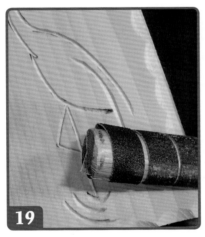

**19**

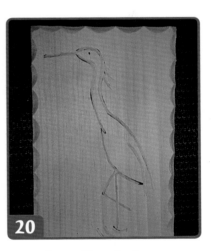

**20**

Here, the carving is complete.

Rather than leaving the edge plain, use the round sanding stick and scallop the edge of the wood.

Here, the scalloped edge is complete.

This carving is far too large for an inkpad, so printer's ink was rolled onto the wood with a brayer and the paper was applied to the wood.

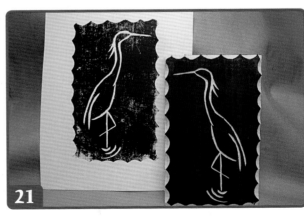

**21**

# CHINESE CHARACTER WOODCUT

## Ages 9 to 12

Chinese character to inspire their students. What could be more appropriate for carvers than the Chinese character for wood?

**1**

**Select a piece of white pine with an area of clear, straight-grained wood at least 4 x 4 x ¾ inches.** Measure a 4 x 4-inch piece, cut it and sand all surfaces.

*(reversed for transfer)*

**Project Pattern**

**Transfer the pattern to the wood.** Be sure to reverse the pattern so that the woodcut stamps the character correctly.

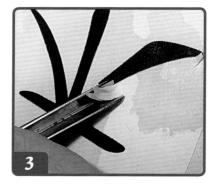

**Start by using the v-tool from the inside of the lines to the outside.** Do not try to get too close to where the lines meet as this will be carved with a knife.

**Pick one of the junctures of the lines and begin a three-cut chip with a stop cut.** Stop cut the other side and use the levering cut to release the chip.

**These two techniques will be repeated to raise the character from the wood.** V-tool around each line. Take care not to carve completely to the point where the lines meet.

**Use the knife where the lines meet and make a three-cut to ensure nice, crisp lines.**

92

Section Five: Woodcuts and Engraving

**7**

**The top of this line can be carved with a single v-tool cut.**

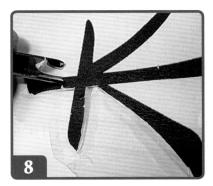

**8**

**Carve down the opposite side.** Carve up to the previous line and make the stop cut to carve out the corner.

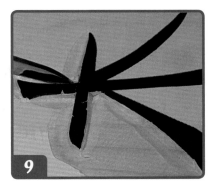

**9**

**Make the second stop cut.** Use a levering cut to release the chip.

**10**

**In this case, start with the stop cut.** Cut the second stop cut.

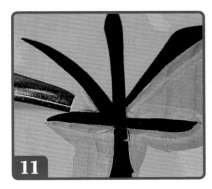

**11**

**Make the levering cut.**

Carve up to the juncture of the lines with the v-tool. Repeat the v-tool work on the other side of the line.

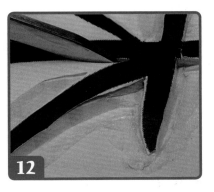

**12**

**Yet again, another 3-cut.** Stop cut one side.

**13**

**Use a levering cut to finish the three-cut.**

**14**

**Begin the last three-cut.**

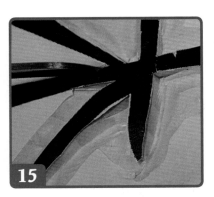

**15**

**The second knife cut.**

**16**

The last levering cut.

**17**

Carefully v-tool up the right side of the last line.

**18**

**After v-tooling the end of the line, carve up to the three-cut again.** Then v-tool up to the last line of the stamp.

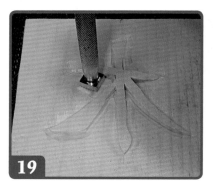

**19**

Use a toothed stamp to recess the rest of the wood around the character.

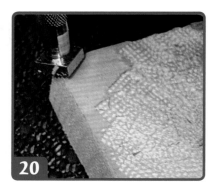

**20**

Lower all the sides more clearly so they don't show up in the stamp.

**21**

The completed stamp.

**22**

Ink up the stamp and try it out.

# LIBRARY BOOKPLATE

## Ages 13 and up

My younger daughter Kathleen (who prefers to be called Kat) inspired this library plate. It's just the right size to mark her copies of the book series she is currently reading. With luck, this stamp will enhance the chances that the earlier books in the series will find their way back to her when her friends finish reading them.

**Project Pattern**

**Select a piece of wood about 5 x 8 x ¾ inches.** Transfer the pattern onto the wood. Keep in mind that the image needs to be reversed so that the block will print correctly.

**Begin with the ⅜-inch v-tool and carve the line of the box around the image.** Although this task is easier using a v-tool, if one is not available it can be accomplished with a knife. Make a stop cut along the center of the line. Then insert the knife at an angle to the stop cut and carve free a long chip. Turn the carving around and do the same in the other direction. Whatever the method used, at the end the box around the image should be carved to an even depth. Use a ⅜-inch #9 gouge to lower and remove the wood outside of the box just carved to a depth of about ¼ inch. If necessary, use the v-tool to sharpen up the lines of the box.

**Here the knife could be used to cut in the letters, but if a v-tool is available the lines may look more consistent.**

**4**

**In this photo, the first letter is completed.** Some of the letters will be more easily carved if they are done in segments. For example all four legs of this letter "X" were carved from the end of each leg into the center. Proceed on to the other letters using the v-tool.

**5**

**When the first line is completed, go to the bottom and carve the letters of the name.**

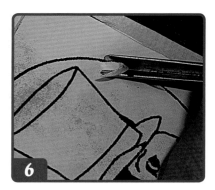

**6**

**Using the v-tool, carve a line around the inside of the oval of the cat.** The v-tool can be leaned in toward the waste wood inside the oval.

**7**

**The next group of steps entails making 3-cut chips into every corner that needs to be "white," or lower.** Here, we make a first stop cut under the brim of the hat.

**8**

**A second stop cut is made along the face.** Then make an angled cut and the chip will come out. Use this technique to remove the wood between tufts of fur on the cheeks. On each side, start with the lowest of the three tufts. Make a stop cut along the face, another along the tuft, and then a levering cut up to the face.

**9**

**Turn the carving around and remove a chip from between the ear and the hat.** Turn the carving back, and remove a chip from the other side.

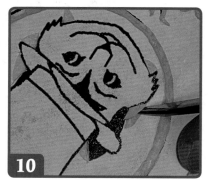

**10**

**Turn back again to the other side.** Cut a wide triangle to define where the face becomes the ear.

**11**

**Separate the ear from the lower part of the brim of the hat.**

**12**

**Then separate the ear from the upper part of the hat brim.**

**13**

Carve the outline of the top hat.

**14**

Continue around the entire outline of the cat and hat.

**15**

Rather than carve the details of the tufts of fur on either side of the face with the v-tool, carve around them, leaving the wood.

**16**

Using the bench knife again, deepen the cuts, using the same three-cut technique. With the v-tool, carve in the cat's mouth starting with the smile.

**17**

When the mouth is complete, carve the lines for the nose with the same tool.

**18**

Carve the eyebrow lines with the v-tool; then carve the outline of the eyes. Cautiously, carve in the pupil using the v-tool.

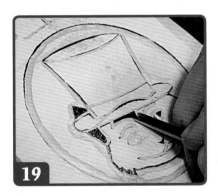

**19**

Outline the hair with the v-tool.

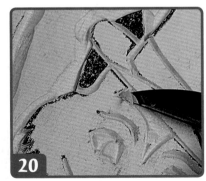

**20**

**The hair will be white, so it needs to be lowered.** Take out the wood from the three corners using a three-cut for each. Plan them correctly and all the hair will be lowered.

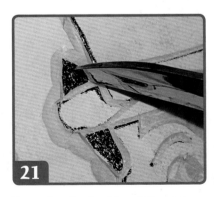

**21**

To make the inside of the ear white, make another three-cut, with the stop cuts parallel to the sides of the ear.

**22**

The second stop cut is into unsupported wood, so proceed carefully.

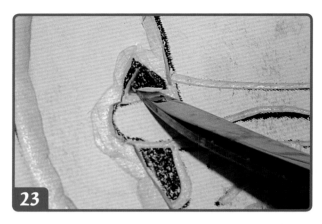

**23**

It will be safer to make the levering cut toward the side of the ear closest to the hat. Perform the same cuts for the lower part of the ear.

**24**

Use a ¾-inch #3 or #5 gouge to lower the wood between the outline around the cat and the inside of oval.

**25**

You may find it helpful once an area is lowered to go around the inside of the oval with a small #9 or #11 gouge, or a v-tool, so that the edge is smooth.

**26**

Here, the carving work is completed.

**27**

If you used an adhesive to attach the pattern, be careful not to scratch the wood when you remove the paper. This woodcut is too large for an inkpad, so I used a brayer to roll ink onto the block. Once there was sufficient ink on the block, I placed it, inked side up, on the bench and pressed a clean sheet of paper onto it. It helps to rub the back of the paper a bit to produce a good transfer.

# MAKING A CHOP

## Ages 13 and up

In the East, chops are functional as signatures but the finest examples are prized as works of art.

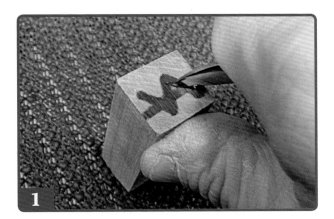

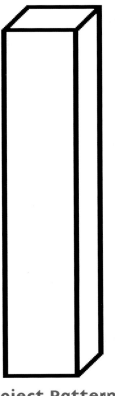

**Project Pattern**

**Select and cut a piece of hardwood ¾ x ¾ x 3 inches.** Fruitwoods like apple and cherry work best, but any tight-grained wood will work. Sand all surfaces, especially the ends, which need to be very flat and smooth. A piece this small should be secured in a vice.

Transfer the character to the end grain wood, reversed. In this case, a stylized "R" was chosen. Most of the initial work is using three-cuts to remove triangular chips from the corners. Start with the inside of the top of the letter "R" and make a stop cut.

**Stop cut along the other side inside the "R."**

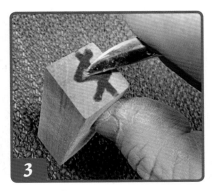

**Use a levering cut to remove the chip from the center.** At the bottom of the "R," make another stop cut along the vertical line.

Make the second stop cut under the diagonal line.

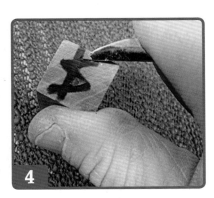

**A levering cut from the vertical line to the diagonal will release the chip.**

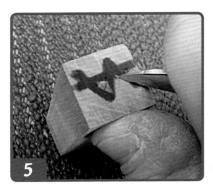

**5**

**Above the diagonal line, make the first stop cut.** Then make the second stop cut opposite of the first.

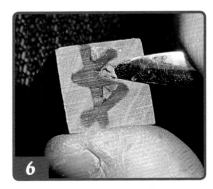

**6**

**Another levering cut removes the wood between the two stop cuts.**

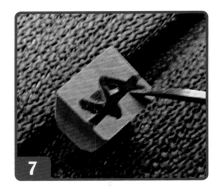

**7**

**On the back of the "R," start another three-cut with a stop-cut.** The second cut goes along the vertical line.

**8**

**The third cut, the levering cut, starts at the second cut and carves up to the first.**

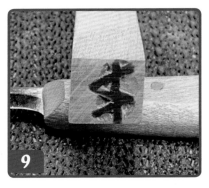

**9**

**Continue these same techniques until all the corners are complete.** Deepen the earlier three-cuts with levering cuts to raise the letter further. Work your way around the entire letter. Continue, as the letter becomes visibly free of the wood. Using stop cuts, re-define the sharp lines of the original pattern. Use controlled cuts to shave down the outside of the stamp.

**10**

**Here, the stamp is completed.**

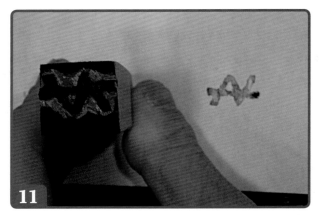

**11**

**The completed chop and an example of the stamp it can make.**

# A WOODCUT SCENE

## Ages 13 and up

The sea and those who derive their livelihood from it are popular subjects for art here in New England. The fisherman in the pattern is based on a sketch I made some years ago and shared with some woodcarvers. Ivan Whillock was kind enough not only to provide me with a helpful critique, but carved his interpretation of the fisherman and sent it to me as a gift.

**Project Pattern**

**Choose a piece of straight-grained white pine at least 6 x 9 x ¾ inches.** Transfer the pattern to the wood.

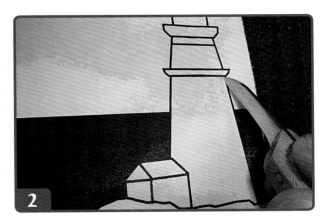

**Start with the lighthouse.** The black lines need to be left to make the print. The first step is to take a three-cut chip out of every corner of the lighthouse drawing. Make the first stop cut inside and along the right side of the bottom of the lighthouse.

*(left)* **Make the second stop cut under, and across, the first landing of the lighthouse.** Then lever out the chip. Continue this technique wherever you can find a corner in the drawing of the lighthouse.

If the corners are close enough you can extend the length of the stop cuts so that when you are finished cutting into both corners they are connected and the drawn line is raised. Try to complete all the inside corners first.

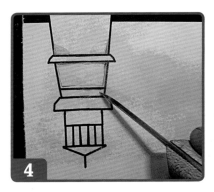

**4**

To carve these slender areas, modify the three-cut process slightly. First make two angled stop cuts from the middle of the narrow area into the corners. Then make the same stop cuts on the other side of the narrow area.

**5**

Make a long stop cut between the points of the earlier stop cuts. Insert the knife tip at one of the corners at an angle and pare toward the other corner. A single chip should be released.

**6**

Flip the knife and cut the bottom, long chip the same way. Remove the tiny triangular chips on the ends and this section is complete.

**7**

Due to the shape of the second landing, you will need to make three stop cuts on each side: one into the upper corner, one into the angled bend, and another into the bottom corner. Lever out the two small triangular chips, then the two long ones as before.

**8**

This section is rectangular and can be carved with a total of five stop cuts and four levering cuts.

**9**

You can see in this picture that while the wood that will be inked is quite narrow, the wood supporting it is triangular. This triangular shape provides strength to the thin lines.

**10**

The windowpanes are thin rectangles and can be carved as before, using five stop cuts and four levering cuts.

**11**

The roof is a triangle. A six-cut carves it out nicely.

**12**

Carve out the right lower corner of the lighthouse where it meets the irregular line of the ground. Then carve the opposite corner where the houselike structure is attached. Cut out the corner where the roof of the houselike structure meets the lighthouse. Although the bottom of the rectangle is not straight, the same nine-cut process can be used here as with the other rectangles. Make stop cuts from the center into each of the corners and then connect them with a longer stop cut.

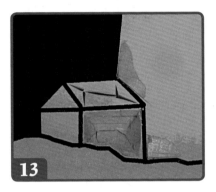

**13**

**Lever out all four chips and then start on the roof.** Since it is a parallelogram, the middle stop cut will be at an angle.

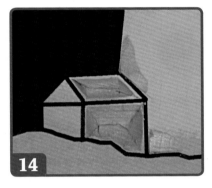

**14**

**When the chips are removed, the roof will resemble the photo.** The side is a triangle and a simple six-cut will remove the necessary wood.

**15**

**The square of the final wall of the houselike structure gets four stop cuts, starting from the center and extending out to each corner.** Lever out the four chips as before.

**16**

**With the houselike structure completed, the corners on the outside of the lighthouse can be carved.** Start with the corner where the lighthouse meets the ocean. Then carve out the opposite side.

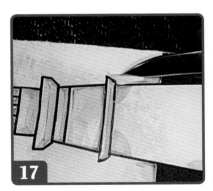

**17**

**If the stop cut on the outside of the first landing is made long enough, it will connect with the cut out areas where the lighthouse meets the ocean.** Be sure to do both sides.

**18**

**Use the same process to remove the wood between the first and second landings.**

  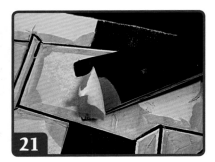

**Once more, carve out the corner, this time above the first landing.** Be sure to preserve the overhang of the roof when carving out that corner. The wood on either side of the spire can be removed using triangular six-cuts. This will leave the spire strong when we remove the background wood.

**Using a ⅜-inch v-tool, carve the inside lines of the base of the lighthouse.** Then carve the irregular line of the ground under the lighthouse.

**Using a ¾- inch #3 gouge, remove the wood inside the lower part of the lighthouse.** Also, carve the wood from above the second landing.

 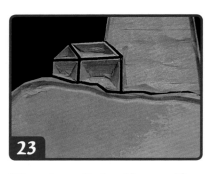 

**Using the v-tool, carve under the irregular line where the ground meets the lighthouse.**

**When done, it should resemble the photo above.**

**Just as we carve the lighthouse, we will look for corners and simple shapes that can be chip-carved from the fisherman's head and surrounding area.** Start at the corner beneath the eyebrow where it meets the ocean. Then carve the corners out from under each lock of hair that sticks out from under the hat.

**Remove the chip between the hair and the hat.** Then proceed to the top of the hat and remove a chip from the corner where the turned up part of the hat meets the top. Turning the piece around, carve out the triangular area where the hat flops back.

Remove a longer triangular chip from where the hat folds to the corner where the turned-up part of the hat meets the top. Then remove a chip between the hat and the ocean.

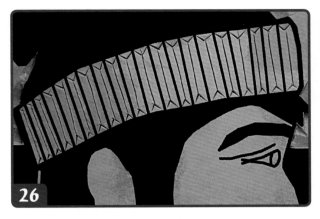

**The pattern of the hat is a series of small rectangles.** You will find this work will go easier if you do all the stop cuts first. Then do all the levering cuts. When done, this will raise up the lines on the turned up area of the hat so that they will take the ink.

**The collar of the sweater can be carved using the same method as the bottom of the hat.** Make all of the stop cuts first, then make the levering cuts.

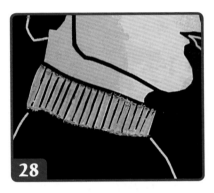

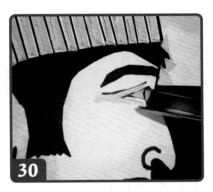

**When completed, the collar should resemble the photos.**

**Begin the facial details with the eye.** The corner of the eye is essentially another triangle, so a three-cut can be used. Make two stop cuts working from the corner of the eye towards the iris. The wrinkle above the eye can be raised at the same time as the line for the upper eyelid. Carve a line between them using a v-tool.

**Again using the v-tool, carve beneath the line for the lower eyelid.** Lastly for the eye, use the v-tool to remove the wood between the front of the eye and the bridge of the nose.

*(right)* **Carve out the triangular section at the end of the nose.** Be sure to curve the stop cuts in the correct directions, so the end of the nose does not appear too sharp in the prints.

Connect the end of the nose to the eye area using a v-tool cut.

**The progress this far.**

**33**

Keeping the v-tool in hand, carve the hairline from the sideburn, up and around the forehead and connect to the three-cut made over the eyebrow.

**34**

Line up the v-tool with one of the splits in the hair at the bottom of the sideburn. Press the v-tool into the wood. Repeat for all of the splits. Use a knife tip for levering cuts. With the v-tool go around the bottom of the sideburn and the inside of the ear.

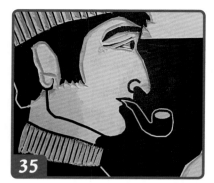

**35**

The corner under the earlobe can be carved out now. Remove the triangular shape on the other side of the jawline under the ear, as well. When complete the project should resemble the photograph.

**36**

Carve out the chip at the bottom of the hairline and another where the neck meets the collar of the sweater. Next, chip-carve out the corners under the jaw line and where the neck meets the sweater.

**37**

Using the V-tool, carve above the line of the sweater and below the line of the jaw.

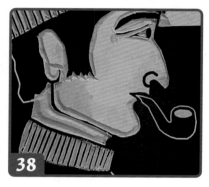

**38**

When the neck area is lined in, use the v-tool to carve above the line for the jaw between the pipe all the way back to the ear.

**39**

Remove the triangular area that will form the lower lip. Then do the same for the upper lip. Another two stop cuts and a levering cut will clear the corner where the lip meets the nostril.

**40**

The fisherman should resemble this photo.

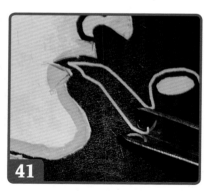

**41**

White lines in the pattern can be carved in with a v-tool. In the corner above the nostril is a small triangle that can also be carved out. Raise the nostril line by carving along both of its sides.

**42**

Still using the v-tool, outline the outside of the hat. Carve the horizon line using the v-tool.

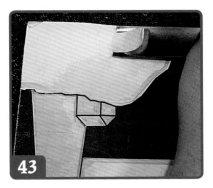

**43**

Use a ¾-inch-wide #3 gouge to lower the white areas.

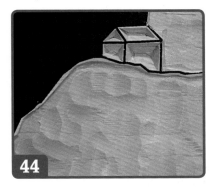

**44**

All these areas of the wood must be lower than the black areas or it will mar the print.

**45**

After the wood of the cliff, lower the wood for the sky. It need not be perfectly smooth, but it must be lower than the black lines and areas. Remove what you can with the larger tool, being careful not to carve off the details.

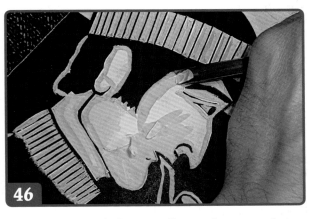

**46**

As necessary, switch to smaller or deeper tools to get the white areas lower than the black. The bowl of the pipe can be carved out with a smaller #9 or #11 tool. Cut an oval from one side, turn the carving and then carve from the other direction to release a single oval shaped chip.

**47**

At this point, our woodcut is ready for ink.

**48**

A woodcut like this can produce many prints before the details start to wear off. Try it on different kinds of paper or with permanent ink on textiles.

# SECTION SIX: BONUS PATTERNS

*These patterns are provided as an inspiration for further projects.*
*The carver may choose to carve them in the round, make relief*
*carvings, create woodcuts, or use them as ornamentation on*
*decorative platters.*

The Old Man

Flying Dove

Unicorn

Nativity Scene

Angel

Mr. Windy
Beard

Marching
Soldier

Mother and
Infant

Poinsettia

# More Great Woodworking Books from Linden Publishing

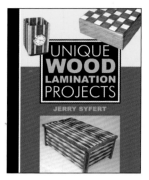

*Unique Wood
Lamination Projects*
88 pp. $19.95
978-0-941936-88-0

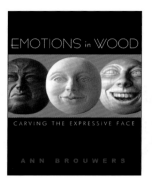

*Emotions in Wood:
Carving the
Expressive Face*
128pp. $19.95
978-1-933502-16-8

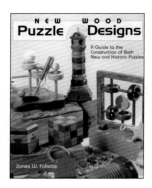

*New Wood
Puzzle Designs*
96pp. $21.95
978-0-941936-57-6

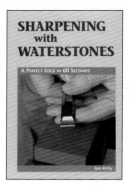

*Sharpening with Waterstones:
A Perfect Edge in 60 Seconds*
96pp. $14.95
978-0-941936-76-7

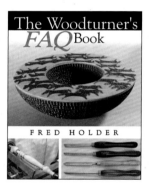

*The Woodturners
FAQ Book*
126pp. $19.95
978-0-941936-94-1

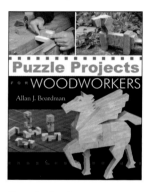

*Puzzle Projects
for Woodworkers*
96pp. $19.95
978-1-933502-11-3

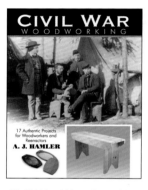

*Civil War Woodworking*
164pp. $24.95
978-1-933502-28-1

*The Art of Whittling*
91pp. $9.95
978-1-933502-07-6

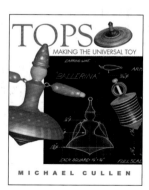

*Tops: Making the
Universal Toy*
128pp. $17.95
978-1-933502-17-5

*Carving for Kids*
104pp. $16.95
978-1-933502-02-1

*How to Choose
and Use Bench Planes*
110pp. $21.95
978-1-933502-29-8

*Speed Toys for Boys*
96 pp. $12.95
978-1933502-18-2

110